IT HAPPENED TO ME

Series Editor: Arlene Hirschfelder

Books in the It Happened to Me series are designed for inquisitive teens digging for answers about certain illnesses, social issues, or lifestyle interests. Whether you are deep into your teen years or just entering them, these books are gold mines of up-to-date information, riveting teen views, and great visuals to help you figure out stuff. Besides special boxes highlighting singular facts, each book is enhanced with the latest reading lists, websites, and an index. Perfect for browsing, there are loads of expert information by acclaimed writers to help parents, guardians, and librarians understand teen illness, tough situations, and lifestyle choices.

AUTISM SPECTRUM DISORDER

THE ULTIMATE TEEN GUIDE

FRANCIS TABONE

IT HAPPENED TO ME, NO. 50

ROWMAN & LITTLEFIELD
Lanham • Boulder • New York • London

Published by Rowman & Littlefield
A wholly owned subsidiary of The Rowman & Littlefield Publishing Group, Inc.
4501 Forbes Boulevard, Suite 200, Lanham, Maryland 20706
www.rowman.com

Unit A, Whitacre Mews, 26-34 Stannary Street, London SE11 4AB

British Library Cataloguing in Publication Information Available

Library of Congress Cataloging-in-Publication Data

Names: Tabone, Francis, 1965– author.
Title: Autism spectrum disorder : the ultimate teen guide / Francis Tabone.
Description: Lanham : Rowman & Littlefield, [2016] | Series: It happened to me ; no. 50 | Includes bibliographical references and index.
Identifiers: LCCN 2016000780 (print) | LCCN 2016001778 (ebook) | ISBN 9781442262416 (hardback : alk. paper) | ISBN 9781442262423 (electronic)
Subjects: LCSH: Autism spectrum disorders—Popular works. | Teenagers—Life skills guides.
Classification: LCC RC553.A88 T33 2016 (print) | LCC RC553.A88 (ebook) | DDC 616.85/88200835—dc23
LC record available at http://lccn.loc.gov/2016000780

To the memory of Oliver Sacks.

Dr. Sacks was a pioneer in understanding and appreciating the diversity of the human mind.

His work led the charge in broadening human awareness and appreciation of those with differences.

Contents

Preface

As the last words of the book were put to paper, an article came out stating that one in forty-five people is now identified with autistic spectrum disorder (ASD).[1] This study reports the highest incidence to date of ASD. For the past several years the number had been around one in sixty-eight; prior to that 1 in about 150. As the numbers grow more questions emerge. Why is ASD becoming more prevalent? Are there more cases, or are we just more aware of these individuals? This new study used parent questionnaires to gain the information. Prior research had used actual diagnostic information based on medical data. So for now the official number is still one in sixty-eight, but that may not stay official for long.

Every day it seems there are new studies, new information, and new theories about ASD. It is hard to keep up with the topic, and even harder to know what to believe. A condition so common is going to gain a lot of attention, with many differing opinions. The point of this book is to give you the most relevant information and to help you understand the past, present, and future regarding ASD. The hope is that after reading this book, you will walk away better educated about the topic and will better understand the conversation at large.

Perhaps you have a sibling or friend with ASD or perhaps you have been diagnosed with ASD. In either case, this book will serve as a resource to better understand not only what ASD is but how society reacts and adapts to this population.

ASD is relatively new (believe it or not). It is not that the condition is new, but the term *autistic spectrum disorder* has only been applied since 2015. Prior to 2015, one might have been diagnosed with autism, Asperger's syndrome, or pervasive developmental disorder (all of which will be discussed in this book). Now we use the term *autism spectrum disorder* for all of these diagnoses. This new way of classifying people with ASD describes a wide variety of behaviors, making it difficult to understand what ASD is and what an individual with ASD is like; it is just too big a group to effectively put into a neat category.

ASD, being so common, drives researchers to look for a cause. To date, there is nothing that directly leads to what causes ASD; in fact the more that is learned, the more questions there are. Scientists are actively trying to figure out the details that add up to ASD.

But as there is a desire to understand, it is important not to lose sight of the fact that people with ASD are here, now, and we may learn a lot through our

Knowledge Is Power

You will most likely meet someone with ASD. You may share a class or work space with someone who has been diagnosed with ASD. The more you know about ASD, the more you will benefit from sharing experiences with those who are different from you.

Diversity in the classroom leads to better understanding among all students. © *Thinkstock*

Students who share a classroom with someone with ASD report an increased understanding and acceptance of diversity. It helps students develop more empathy and respect for all people. Sharing a classroom or work space with someone with ASD creates opportunities to master activities and school work by teaching concepts to and practicing concepts with a fellow student or coworker with ASD. It even leads to better academic outcomes for those students without ASD.[a]

interactions with those who belong to this community. Those with ASD have tremendous gifts that help all people better understand the human experience. Those who are different help us to reflect on the basic elements of ourselves.

With the new numbers (unofficial for now) reporting that one in forty-five (or 2 percent) of the population is someone with ASD, it is essential that education be available to help the world become more aware and knowledgeable about the subject. If you are in a school with 500 students, chances are there are ten individuals with ASD. Those ten students need to be included not excluded from the school community. This starts with education and awareness for the other 490 students in the school.

Acknowledgments

Writing a book on autistic spectrum disorder requires the input of the families and students I have worked with over the past thirty years. I thank them for their contributions and their generosity in sharing their stories within these pages. It is a gift to work with them. They have been essential in my work and continue to inspire.

In addition, those educators who have helped to shape my career are invaluable in this process. My great thanks to Sid Massey, Dr. Michael Termini, and Mary Clancy for helping to shape my path in the world of special education. From these people I have learned a great deal about education, social justice, and life in general. They have shaped my work and provided the guidance I needed to fulfill my educational journey. They have helped me to see the necessity of empowering those with special needs with independence through education. Their work has helped me to form the words and structure of this book.

My wife, Karen, continues to be the most important person in getting this book together. She has been my best advocate and friend in addition to providing so much of the technical assistance needed to write this book. I thank her for her support and patience.

Finally, I thank my daughter, Camille. Until you are a parent, advice on parenting is easy to give. It was Camille who gave me the reality check that until you raise a child yourself, you don't really know as much about children as you think you do. She has inspired me to better understand the concerns, questions, and excitement all parents experience in their child-rearing journey.

AN INTRODUCTION TO ASD

Many years ago, when I was in high school, we had a few students who stood out from the rest. Like many stories I have heard since, all high schools seemed to have one or two kids whose behavior was odd and often disruptive—not enough to keep them out of a typical school, but enough that they would either be ostracized or "egged on" by peers to produce behavior disruptive to the routines of the day.

For example, I knew a young man we called Chicken Joe, or CJ. He was about two years older than me and I never really got to meet him face-to-face, but CJ would suffer the constant barrage of kids asking him, "What you choking Joe?" His response was always the same, "Choking the chicken!" and he would explode in laughter and end up grabbing his private parts and imitating masturbation in the hallway. This in turn would get the students riled up in a never-ending circle of teasing. In the cafeteria students would also begin the chant of "Go CJ, Go CJ," to which he would jump on the table and pretend to masturbate. The inevitable result was CJ being led into the office to cool down. He rarely said anything else. I only saw him a few times in class, head down in a book, or in the hallways, his fingers wildly flapping next to his eyes. Truthfully, I didn't understand anything other than CJ was a weird kid. He seemed to enjoy the egging by students, but I couldn't help but wonder if people were being mean or if they were in some way setting CJ free to act out this odd behavior. He seemed so happy most of the time. I look back and see how dreadfully wrong the students were to instigate this disruptive and inappropriate behavior.

My real education about these "stand-out" students was meeting a young man named Chris. Chris and I were in the same grade in high school and took a few classes together. We shared classes like shop and art, gym, and a music class, but academically he was in every advanced placement class. I, on the other hand, was barely getting through my routine of regular classes. Chris was odd, no doubt, but he didn't get egged on like CJ; he was more of a loner but still subject to the less-than-civil behavior of other classmates. He walked the halls with his books tightly gripped to his chest with his head down, moving so fast he'd bump into

Trying to Fit In

Researchers from the Kennedy Krieger Institute in Baltimore and Johns Hopkins University conducted a survey of over a thousand parents who had a child with an autism spectrum disorder diagnosis. The results found that 63 percent of the kids had been bullied. The researchers also found these children were three times more likely to be bullied than their siblings who did not have autism.[a]

School is a difficult place for those who don't fit in. © *Thinkstock*

almost everyone. I would later learn that kids would try and knock down his books. His response would be a high-pitched whine, and he'd yell at the perpetrator, "No! You are not to do that! It's wrong, it's wrong." He'd need a moment to stop rocking, and then collect his books and move on. He was also fond of lecturing other students about their behavior. In the classes we did share, he'd often correct other students by saying, "You didn't raise your hand," or "Ooooooooooo" when another student failed to turn in an assignment.

My better understanding of Chris came with a slap in the face. I wasn't a bad student, just a lazy one, who spent more time in the school's parking lot hanging out with friends than going to class. I didn't really get in any trouble but had a few bad habits. One of those habits was sneaking cigarettes in the boy's bathroom (a terrible habit I have since removed from my routine). So as I was pulling the last puff of a cigarette, Chris walked into the bathroom. Upon seeing me exhale the smoke, he walked over, smacked me in the face, pulled the lit cigarette from my lips, and crushed it on the floor. Then he shook a nagging finger in my face and lectured about the ills of breaking school rules.

I stood in shock. "He smacked me in the face," I thought. "I am going to punch his lights out." I didn't. Instead I looked at him and said, "You are right Chris." I was fuming inside (irrationally, of course) but realized something bigger was going on with this kid. Maybe he was weird or odd, but there was something more to being weird or odd. I started to piece together what I had seen from him before, an unwavering adherence to school rules as well as making sure everyone else was also following the rules.

A few days after the slap I was in the library with friends. We'd have a study hall certain days. If we wanted to work in the library, we'd have to sign a sheet in our study hall class. The group would then add a few fake names like Pete Moss, Jim Nasium, Mya Butreeks, and so on. When the librarian would read the names aloud, we would all giggle and get sent back to study hall class, denied entrance to the library. On this particular day, Chris sat down with us. Uninvited, he squeezed between two of us in what was space enough for two. As the librarian began to read the list, I panicked. I knew this would send Chris into a tizzy. I really did get nervous. I broke into a sweat knowing he was going to smack someone or start screaming about the rules.

Well, this time the librarian had enough. After reading the fake names, he blew his top and sent us all to the principal, Chris included. Chris wailed and wailed. Regardless of us trying to calm him down he cried mercilessly and began to slap himself. Even the librarian couldn't get him to stop. We never made it to the principal and spent the next hour trying to calm Chris down.

There were four of us at the table that day—Chris, myself, and two friends. One of my friends, James, was a notoriously bad student and troublemaker. Wearing cutoff shirts and a leather vest, he was clearly no one to mess with, and as his facial hair came in he looked even tougher. He had a reputation as being a drug dealer connected to the "mob" (which was untrue, but he liked the tag) and as having many other run-ins with the law. It was a few weeks later when I saw my tough friend helping Chris pick up his books after someone had knocked them to the ground. Chris's next three years became much easier. Knowing Chris had a friend as tough as James kept the wolves at bay. Chris usually hung around with us in the cafeteria or yard. We tolerated him. He was odd, said weird things, and often repeated things over and over. When eating he'd take huge bites and barely chew. He would want to talk about classical instruments and the sounds they made. Chris played bassoon, an instrument that added to his weirdness. None of us ever had heard of such an instrument.

Chris and I ended up going to the same local community college, both enrolled in the music program. Chris was serious about music; I was not. I hung out (again) in the college cafeteria with my music school friends (all of us knowing nothing about classical music; we were only there because we thought we'd end up as rock stars). Chris once again joined the group. I introduced him and pointed out that while strange, he was an interesting person. I soon learned that in addition to his gifted academic knowledge, he had perfect pitch. This meant upon hearing a series of notes, he could name them perfectly. When asked to sing an F-sharp, he did it immediately. His hearing and pitch were amazing. People would ask him to sing the entire bassoon part for Beethoven's Fifth or other massive works of music. To which he did. He became an instant celebrity in the cafeteria.

I lost touch with Chris. Knowing him was a real eye-opener in terms of the disparity between someone's cognitive ability and social skills. Chris was smart with the books, but when it came to his social skills, he couldn't get through a conversation without interrupting or saying something that someone would interpret as rude. He overreacted to almost every joke we told, or if we'd make a rude comment, he would lecture us for an endless amount of time.

I remember in high school asking a teacher the rude question, "What is wrong with him?" Today I would ask a different question, "Why is his behavior so contrary to general social norms?" I also remember the teacher saying to me, "I don't know; he has social issues."

I learned about autism spectrum disorder from CJ and Chris early on. I was more interested in them than in making fun of them or egging on behavior I knew most kids thought was funny. I wanted to understand their world, their inflexibility, their sensory needs (Chris would eat without breathing), and most importantly why Chris could sing a B-flat without blinking, knew every chemical element's atomic weight, but couldn't understand a simple joke.

I would later learn more about autism and autism spectrum disorder, pervasive developmental disorder, and Asperger's syndrome, names that would have been used to describe CJ and Chris. Back then most people had no idea what made these individuals special. Focus was more on those who were nonverbal or detached from any social conversations.

Many years later I worked with students with emotional disabilities. Teaching fourth through sixth grade students with behavioral issues was a challenge. Ralphie was the first student I ever met who actually had a diagnosis of autism. Unlike the other students, Ralphie was more introverted in his behavior. He spoke to himself; he would say things he heard on the subway over and over (echolalia). Ralphie would freeze in a position and not move. He would ask the same questions over and over, often anticipating one's answer.

I taught Ralphie in the fifth grade. Realizing he needed a specialized setting, I found him a more appropriate placement in a new program; however, the new assigned school sent him back stating that it couldn't work with him. Even though I worked in a class that taught the sixth grade, he came back to my class in the sixth, seventh, and eighth grades. The school system was a failure in finding an appropriate placement for Ralphie that was conducive to his learning and social/emotional support.

CJ, Chris, and Ralphie represent a small part of the continuum called autism spectrum disorder. These three young men were very different, but all had social difficulties that impaired their general functioning in everyday situations. That was pretty much all they had in common. While Chris was reading chemistry manuals, Ralphie never read at anything higher than a second grade level. Ralphie was prone to aggressive outbursts, whereas Chris would cry hysterically when upset. As my career grew, I learned much more about autism and autism spectrum disorder. I soon began to realize that there was a core of behaviors that were certainly deficits (social interactions, language abilities, daily living skills) this group shared, but there were vast differences among the individuals.

Since 2015, the term *autism spectrum disorder* (ASD) been used to characterize this wide range of students. The term *spectrum* implies an underlying structure that results in a range of functioning. For example, those diagnosed with ASD may range from having no verbal skills to having seemingly normal language skills. One may have no ability to socialize (not even make eye contact), some may have minor interactions, and others may socialize like Chris. How is it that this one term can describe the millions worldwide who share the diagnosis? A good question that will be examined in this book.

ASD is classified as a mental disorder that impairs social communication and social interaction, and includes repetitions of patterns of behavior, interests, and activities. ASD must be evident in the early stages of life and impair one's ability in social, occupational, or other areas of one's life. It is not a "neat" disorder. The variability of symptoms among people is incredibly diverse. Some people with ASD have communication deficits that render them unable to communicate, while others can have typical conversations. Thus the term *spectrum* suggests that this is a disability with a huge range of symptoms.

ASD has a short history in the mental health field. Its popularity has grown exponentially in the last twenty years. With an increased incidence and global attention, there has been much research and study of the topic. Having read as much of the literature as I can, I have surmised several points regarding what the current scientific community thinks about ASD.

First, I read a lot about how we are "close" to understanding the cause of ASD or more specifically why it develops. It seems that with each layer of scientific advancement comes a better understanding. As technology improves we get better pictures of the brain. We can now watch information (through electrical impulses) move through the brain; thus we can now compare the brains of individuals with and without ASD to help explain why things are the way they are.

Another important element from the literature is that while there are many theories of what causes ASD, they are only best-guess scenarios. There aren't any hard-and-fast rules. There is no smoking gun that says anything in particular definitely causes ASD. This is probably the most frustrating part of the research. As human beings, we have grown in our use of technology, medicine, chemicals, and the creation of agents that seem to have an impact on our environment. While many guess that these things contribute to a rise in ASD, looking for that single agent has proven to be a fruitless search, but it has started some helpful conversations.

Finally, what the literature reports is that the concept of ASD is much bigger than the sum of its parts. Why? When looking at the variables—the individual characteristics of a person with ASD; the genetic, hereditary makeup of the individual; and the growth of each individual—there are no constants. Every person with ASD has his or her own unique makeup, his or her own unique strengths and challenges, and his or her own stories. ASD is not a disease and cannot be treated as one. Instead it is a complex condition that impacts everyone differently, and has no reliable course of treatment. There are only ways to manage the behavior, which will be discussed later in the book.

Essentially, to diagnose ASD some essential definitions are used. First, ASD can result in persistent impairment in reciprocal (back-and-forth) communication and social interaction. These impairments must be apparent at an early age for a diagnosis of ASD. In addition, an individual with ASD has restricted interests and repetitive behaviors. For example, I work with a student who asks me where I am going every day so he can then ask the mode of transportation. While I give the same answer every time, he continues to ask. It isn't just me he asks; he asks almost all those he encounters. When I try to change the conversation, he inevitably winds back to his agenda.

Prior to 2015, ASD was not a single diagnosis. There were many terms to describe different levels of autism. For example, an individual who had social difficulties but did not have any cognitive deficits was diagnosed as a person with Asperger's syndrome. Those individuals with deficits in social, cognitive, and language were diagnosed as individuals with pervasive developmental disorder (PDD) or autism, depending on additional factors. Those individuals previously diagnosed with autism or Asperger's or PDD are now collectively diagnosed with ASD. As you can imagine, using one term to describe all people with social and communication disorders might get confusing because of the variations of behavior among people. Thus, we do use qualifiers to further explain ASD.

Diagnostic Language of ASD

There are a lot of extra words that go into a diagnosis of ASD. These words help to describe the individual's characteristics under the umbrella of the term *ASD*. They also give us a better picture of the types of support the individual may need. For example, one can have three levels of severity attached to the ASD diagnosis. The three categories are an individual with ASD requiring support, an individual with ASD requiring substantial support, and an individual with ASD requiring very substantial support.

Support Descriptions Associated with ASD

Level 1: Requiring Support

Social Communication

Without supports in place, deficits in social communication cause noticeable impairments. The individual has difficulty initiating social interactions, and has clear examples of atypical or unsuccessful response to social initiation of others. The individual may appear to have decreased interest in social interactions. For example, a person who is able to speak in full sentences and engages in communication but whose basic back-and-forth conversation with others fails. The individual's attempts to make friends are odd and typically unsuccessful.

Restricted, Repetitive Behavior

Inflexibility of behavior may cause interference with functioning in one or more contexts. The individual may have difficulty switching between activities. Problems with organization and planning interfere with one's independence.

Level 2: Requiring Substantial Support

Social Communication

The individual has marked deficits in verbal and nonverbal social communication skills. In addition, the individual has social impairments apparent even with supports in place; limited initiation of social interactions; and reduced or abnormal responses to social initiation from others. For example, a person who speaks simple sentences, whose interaction is limited to narrow special interests, and who has markedly odd nonverbal communication.

Restricted, Repetitive Behaviors

The individual demonstrates an inflexibility of behavior, difficulty coping with change, or other restricted/repetitive behaviors that appear frequently enough to be obvious to the casual observer and interfere with functioning in a variety of contexts. This is accompanied with stress and/or difficulty changing focus or action.

Level 3: Requiring Very Substantial Support

Social Communication

The individual has severe deficits in verbal and nonverbal social communication skills that cause severe impairments in functioning. The individual has very limited initiation with social interactions, and minimal response to social initiation from others. For example, a person with few words of intelligible speech who rarely initiates interaction and, when he or she does, makes unusual approaches to meet needs only and responds only to very direct social approaches.

Restricted, Repetitive Behavior

The individual has an inflexibility of behavior, extreme difficulty coping with change, or other restricted/repetitive behavior that markedly interferes with functioning in all spheres. There is great distress/difficulty when changing focus or action.[b]

In addition to the level of severity, a diagnosis needs to specify if there is any intellectual impairment. Many people with ASD have no difficulty with general intellectual pursuits. Of course, some will have difficulty. Thus, in addition to severity, the diagnosis includes either with or without accompanying intellectual impairment.

Following severity, with or without intellectual impairment, there needs to be a statement on whether there is language impairment. This should not be confused with the person's impairment with social communication. Instead, there is a need to identify if there is language production or processing problems. Something like apraxia (a condition where the person cannot form appropriate words) needs to be defined separately; thus with or without accompanying language impairment would be added. If there is a language impairment the specific level of speech production should be added to the diagnosis. For example, a diagnosis may read "ASD with accompanying intellectual impairment and accompanying language impairment (no intelligible speech)."

I know this is a lot of diagnostic information, but if you think about it, the more that is identified and specified about the condition, the better grasp you have of the individual. Many times psychologists or educators use the diagnosis for educational placement or treatment. Thus, the more specific the better. So let's keep going!

Next, a diagnosis needs to add whether there is a known medical, neurological, mental, behavioral, or genetic condition or an environmental factor that exists. Rett syndrome is a genetic disorder that leads to social and communication deficits. Thus, a diagnosis might read "ASD with accompanying intellectual impairment, with accompanying language impairment (no intelligible speech), associated with Rett syndrome."

Finally, the term *with catatonia* might be added. Catatonia is an irregularity with movement (typically immobility) or behavioral irregularities caused from a mental condition. A person may freeze or hold a position for long periods of time.

Catatonia is identified because it looks at one's motor functioning (*motor* meaning movements both large and small). It is concerned with the physical elements of ASD. Catatonia symptoms can appear in many other diagnoses as well. The term is added if at least three of the following symptoms exist:

- Stupor (not actively relating to environment)
- Catalepsy (stuck in a posture that goes against gravity, like keeping your arms up)
- Waxy flexibility (if you moved a person's arm, it would remain in that position until you moved it again)
- Mutism (i.e., no, or very little, verbal response)
- Negativism (i.e., no response to instructions or external stimuli)
- Mannerism (i.e., odd, repetition of normal actions)
- Stereotypy (i.e., repetitive, abnormally frequent, non-goal-directed movements)
- Agitation, not influenced by external stimuli
- Grimacing

- Echolalia (i.e., mimicking another's speech)
- Echopraxia (i.e., mimicking another's movements)

In the end, the hope is to have a long descriptive diagnosis. However, this does not give someone all the information to completely describe the individual. This only scratches the surface of the person. A diagnosis of ASD with accompanying intellectual impairment, with accompanying language impairment (no intelligible speech), helps a professional start on the course of action but will never be able to capture the many aspects of an individual with ASD to describe him or her in detail.

Does It Matter?

What makes ASD so different from other mental or physical issues is that it is not always obvious. When you meet a student with Down syndrome, what is your first reaction? Does it make you nervous or uncomfortable? You are able to instantly notice something is different about this person. The physical characteristics are certainly obvious so you have fair warning to interpret this person's words, actions, or behaviors. With ASD this is not the case. I introduce many people to students with ASD. The first question a student may ask a visitor is, "Where do you live?" or the student may stand very close to a visitor, creating an uncomfortable situation for communicating. Many people react with uncertainty about what to say or do. Every person has a different experience with people with disabilities, but with ASD, behavior may be interpreted wrongly.

I was once standing in line at a drug store ready to make a purchase. In walks a student with ASD I recognize. He stands in the doorway and yells, "Do you have an elevator in here?" When no one answers he yells again. Now, I knew this young man made movies about elevators but had never seen him in the community looking for an elevator to film. The staff in the drug store, of course, had no idea what was going on. They yelled at him to get out. As I saw the situation escalating (the security guard began to escort him), I saw the agitation in my student rise. I quickly walked over and told the guard it was OK, that he was with me. The guard's response was, "Well, get him out of here."

The guard had a reasonable duty to escort the young man out. After all, he did not understand the situation. The young man was tall and handsome, and had no visible appearance that he was a person with ASD. But perhaps with some education and awareness, people may begin to understand that seemingly odd behavior can be handled in a way that is neither demeaning nor physical. I realize this is tough, given the wide range of behavior people with ASD have and given the lack of understanding by the community at large.

So does it matter? All these scientific names and diagnoses that accompany ASD don't help us understand how to interact and work with those whose behavior is different or unusual. I hope that this book helps you to better understand not only the behavioral and mental aspects of ASD but also the needs of those with ASD.

The next two chapters of this book will present the basics, which will help you to understand the world of ASD as it stands now—facts, figures, numbers, and how it is truly a health crisis. The initial chapters will also give you the history of how ASD as a diagnosis has evolved, and who the major players in the fields were. The next two chapters will discuss the brain and how movement of information is different for those with ASD. Together, these four chapters give you the basics for understanding ASD from a historical, psychological, and mental health perspective.

The book will then focus on the needs, treatments, and best approaches to working with those with ASD from both an educational and parenting perspective. When understanding the needs of this group, providing an educational and social program becomes difficult. There are many programs out there that work for some. The methods and curriculum most commonly used will be reviewed.

Finally, the book will then focus on the individuals with ASD. It will present the stories and successes of these teens and adults. In addition, the book will present important information for families and friends and tell the stories of those who have adapted their lives to help those with ASD. I hope their voices will inspire and give you the information to be accepting and understanding of those with ASD. These amazing individuals are all important contributors to our society. But you as a reader are just as important as you begin to accept and understand this unique group. For the betterment of our society, people must begin to not just accept and understand those with ASD. People must appreciate the great gifts and talents inherent to every individual encountered on a daily basis.

THE BASICS

Conditions that were once called autism, Asperger's syndrome, or pervasive developmental disorder are now called autism spectrum disorder. There are good reasons to categorize all these names under a blanket terminology. Chapter 3 will present the history and changes, but the term *autism spectrum disorder*, or ASD, is what will be used going forward. This chapter will present the general characteristics of ASD. The goal is to present an overview of the group we define as individuals with ASD.

Notice the word *individual* is first. General consensus is not to use the terms *autistic person* or *ASD person*. It is important to acknowledge the person first, and the disability later. So most current language would use the phrase "This is a boy [or girl] with ASD." The individual person is recognized first. In this way, the individual traits, unique personality, and individual identity of a person is not lost within an ASD diagnosis.

What the Numbers Say

The numbers regarding ASD are pretty staggering. In the United States of America, one out of sixty-eight people born are diagnosed with ASD. When broken down, the rate is much higher for boys—about one in forty-two as opposed to girls for whom the occurrence is 1 in 189. With 1.5 percent of the population diagnosed with ASD, the focus of ASD in mental health communities and the medical world is no surprise.[1]

ASD occurs worldwide with countries identifying between 1 percent and 2.6 percent (Korea is the highest) of their population as individuals with ASD. The diagnosis does not discriminate between race, ethnicity, or economic background. The basic characteristics of ASD are the same all over the world. As one learns more about ASD, education programs and treatments certainly have advanced and made progress. However, as readers will discover there is still a long way to go.

Most children in the United States are diagnosed after the age of four years. However, most researchers and mental health experts agree that ASD can be diagnosed as early as age two. Most parents report that before the age of one year they notice something wrong with their child. Generally, parents notice vision and hearing issues. Poor eye contact and a lack of response to voices are generally the most common complaints. In addition, most children with ASD do not hit their developmental milestones. A milestone is a time period when some developmental level should be reached. For example, by the age of one year a child should be able to say "ma-ma" or "da-da." At the age of one a child should be taking a few steps or standing while holding on to something. When these milestones are not met, it is always a good idea to have things checked out. In most cases a delay may mean nothing, but the earlier ASD is identified, the better the chance for early intervention and treatment.

Many students with ASD are going to need specialized educational services. This will include the work of a special education teacher, speech and language pathologist, psychologist, occupational therapist (to work on small motor/movement tasks such as writing or getting dressed), and a physical therapist (to work with large motor/movement activities such as running, walking, etc.). Not every individual with ASD receives these services. The balance of what is needed varies greatly from person to person. The more one learns about ASD, the more one sees there is a wide range of needs, strengths, and weaknesses from individual to individual.

For a student with ASD, these services on average cost about $20,000 a year more than general education for other students. The dollar figure is mentioned only to highlight how impactful ASD is on our modern society. From this one can see that the prevalence of ASD is expensive and does require government intervention to help provide services. In 2015 it was estimated that the United States spent approximately $250 billion a year. By 2025 it is estimated to increase to $400 billion.[2] Many of the individuals who need care today will need it for the rest of their lives. In addition, some parents will spend an estimated $40,000 to $60,000 a year in behavioral interventions for their child every year.[3]

Most individuals with ASD have additional mental health issues as well. It is estimated that as many as 70 percent of individuals with ASD have an additional diagnosis. About 40 percent have more than one additional diagnosis.[4] Most commonly associated with ASD is anxiety disorder. Because of the social difficulties of individuals with ASD this makes sense and needs to be treated as well as working on enhancing the social performance of the individual. Approximately half of students with ASD have an intellectual disability as well, which means learning, problem solving, and global comprehension is also difficult. Many speech and language issues exist for those with ASD. Approximately half of those identified with ASD may not develop useable language skills. It has also been reported that 20 percent of individuals with ASD also have some form of psychosis, which means a loss of contact with reality.[5] Historically, an individual could not be diagnosed with attention deficit disorder (ADD) and ASD. Because of recent changes in the way ASD is diagnosed, one can now be diagnosed with ADD and ASD. It is believed that up to 30 percent of individuals with ASD also are diagnosed with ADD.[6]

Symptoms of ASD or other diagnoses may change over time. For example, anxiety in a younger child may fade with age. Many behavioral issues may fade with proper training. As a person gets older, so does his or her experience and ability to learn and grow. Such is the case for those with ASD. Behavioral interventions, medications, and other therapeutic services have tremendous impact on helping a person with ASD live a full life.

Who Is a Person with ASD?

This is the part of the book that is impossible to write. "Who is a person with ASD" suggests that there is a single set of behaviors that would describe the large population of individuals with ASD. This is simply not the case. Every person with ASD is different, unique, and completely unlike anyone else. Sure there are similarities amongst the group, but I cannot stress enough how unique each individual with ASD is when compared to others. The most we can do is cluster specific areas of functioning and describe the overarching elements that would help us diagnose. For example, social functioning is compromised for individuals with ASD. Yet for an individual this may range from social withdrawal to complete social inclusion—two completely opposite ends of a spectrum. Here is a look at the domains most associated with ASD. See if it is possible to sum things up.

Social Functioning

The *Diagnostic and Statistical Manual of Mental Disorders*, fifth edition (*DSM-5*) is the book that psychologists, psychiatrists, and medical personnel use to help understand, categorize, and classify certain mental disorders. It helps professionals put complex types of behavior together to help create categories that are similar enough to have a common thread, thus helping to provide treatment. The *DSM-5* can help outline the areas that impact an individual with ASD.

Social functioning is the most pronounced piece of the ASD puzzle. All individuals with ASD have some impairment in social functioning. In this case, social functioning refers to any interaction with other people. Saying hello, ordering food, having a conversation, playing a team sport, and dancing are all examples of social situations that require an individual not only to navigate his or her emotions, knowledge, and comprehension of the event, but also to understand the other person's emotions, knowledge, and comprehension of the event.

Case Study 1

V is a sixteen-year-old high school student with ASD. He is interested in school and generally follows all directions. V reads very well and can do most math calculations well. He does not seek interactions with other students but does seek out adults within the school. He can do most daily life activities without help. Eating, dressing, and traveling are all things he can do independently.

When asked, "How are you?" V does not generally answer. Instead, his first reply is "I am V." I have worked with his family for many years and will often inquire about his siblings and parents. When I ask, "How is your brother?" the reply is "My brother is named J."

"How is mom?" Reply: "My mom is C."

Rather than replying "fine," "good," or "well" to describe the sibling or parent's state of being, V answers with a concrete statement and gives a name. This simple social transaction is difficult as V cannot access how another person feels or cannot describe the emotional state of his family member.

While much work with V has been done to help answer these questions, it is still an area of difficulty. At this point V can state, "I am fine." But this is something he has been taught. It is not applied to other people in his family, but in a social setting he can respond about himself. As students with ASD are directly taught how to answer basic questions, the hope is for the response to generalize into other similar situations. Over time answering "How are you?" could apply to other people as well.

V has difficulty understanding how to relate information about other people from an outside perspective. He is not able to interpret another person's state of being and talk about the details. This can make introductions difficult. Even when V does say, "I am fine," his intonation and delivery are robotic and without emotion. For V it is never "I'm good" or "I'm OK." It is always "I am fine," with a pronounced accent on all three words.

According to the *DSM-5*, the individual must display persistent deficits in social interaction and communication across different settings and different contexts. Thus, an individual does not have trouble with social situations only in one place (like school or in a restaurant). The difficulties with social situations show up in all or most areas of the individual's life.[7]

The social difficulties are most apparent in reciprocity. In other words, simple back-and-forth conversation. This includes problems entering or exiting a conversation. It also is apparent when discussing things outside the interest of the individual. Many students with ASD have limited interests or areas of conversation they can apply in a social situation. For example, if you are in a conversation with an individual with ASD, it might be difficult to change the subject he introduces. As you begin to talk about something else, the individual may continue to reintroduce his topic. The more you try, the less engaged the individual may be. Many times I have had individuals with ASD walk away from me mid-sentence because they just didn't have an interest in what I was saying (so, don't take it personally).

Entering and exiting a conversation are things you may take for granted. You generally do not walk into someone else's conversation and start talking. For those with ASD, that situation can be tough. Many individuals with ASD will abruptly interrupt a conversation with little regard for what is being discussed. It may appear rude, but remember, they do not mean to be disrespectful; those with ASD have difficulty taking in the perspectives of others. They generally do not understand the social ramifications of interrupting others. These individuals may have difficulty understanding that others can have a conversation that excludes them because they maintain an egocentric view of their world.

Exiting a conversation can be equally difficult for those with ASD. Finishing abruptly and walking away, making a seemingly random statement and walking away, or just lingering after their point is made can be the behavior of individuals with ASD. You and I may understand there is etiquette in conversation that would require you to signal the end of a conversation. For example, when you are on the phone, you don't just hang up without saying good-bye. In this way a "good-bye" means both parties know the conversation is over. Or when you are talking to a friend on the street, you finish with "OK, see you later." These seemingly simple behaviors are not so simple. They require more than just the transfer of information; they require a deeper understanding of social norms, perspective taking, and the realization that both you and the other person are equally engaged in discussion. This is difficult for those with ASD as their own perspective and needs may be all they can interpret at the time. Thus, when the information is communicated, the need is filled and that is that; the person walks away.

Social functioning is not limited to verbal interaction. Nonverbal language and body language are equally important. Think about eye contact. Where are your eyes as you speak with someone? In most cases you make eye contact with the person you speak with. In many cases, people with ASD do not make eye contact with the person addressing them or vice versa. A lack of eye contact has been the subject of research for the ASD community. Historically, a big part of ASD instruction included verbal prompts of "eyes on me," a way for direct instruction to improve gaze. It is not clear why people with ASD do not maintain eye contact during discussion, but as more information emerges, practice changes. For example, some studies have now shown that individuals with ASD might have stronger peripheral vision (the vision that occurs outside of your direct gaze) than head-on gaze. So perhaps they are receiving better visual input when not making eye contact.[8] If this is the case, educators should probably not be saying "eyes on me."

Philip Talks about Making Eye Contact

In his blog titled *Faith Hope and Love . . . with Autism*, Philip, a twelve-year-old student with ASD, responds to a question about eye contact presented by the uncle of a person with ASD:

I am letting you know about eye contact. My eyes see very well. Most people seem to need to have to look long and hard to make sense of a picture. I can take in a whole picture at a glance. Each day I see too many little petty details. I look away to not get overwhelmed by a lot of little bits of information. I watch things that a teacher or person I listen to tells me to watch. This helps me concentrate on what I should be focusing on. I can search for a teacher's voice to try to focus on. I am academically learning best when I sit side-by-side with a teacher. A seat on the side keeps me focused on your voice and not on visual distractions. I am assessing many sounds too. I have to erase some stimuli to access my answers to people's questions and meet their demands. That is why I don't make eye contact. I am always listening. I listen a lot to voices. I so love when people talk to me and are not talking like I am not there. I am active because I am unable to feel my body well. People think I am being rude but I can't help it. I need to move to feel my body, but sitting down at least helps me not walk away from you. Please peacefully talk to your nephew. Let him know you understand. I am sad when people think I don't like them. I love people.[a]

Other research has pointed to the fact that at times, visual processing can be overwhelming for the person with ASD. You may have heard about people with photographic memory. They can see an image and instantly remember all the details. What if this was the case for those with ASD that a continuous flood of images with hundreds and thousands of details could not be ignored? This would quickly become overwhelming. Thus, it is proposed that some individuals with ASD do not look directly at the speaker because it is too overwhelming. It may be that the movement of the mouth when one is speaking cannot be ignored, which would interfere with their ability to pay attention, so they look away to be able to listen without the visual input.[9]

Other body language includes standing a comfortable distance away from the person you may be speaking with. For those with ASD, judgment of what constitutes a "comfortable distance" can be impaired. There are many individuals with ASD who stand very close to another person; there are others who stand too far away. In either case it seems that these individuals have difficulty maintaining a space in relation to another that would be considered comfortable to you and me.

Sensory integration is a term we will investigate later on in the book, but it refers to one's ability to input sensory information to produce an appropriate output. For example, you touch a hot stove and you pull back quickly. For someone whose sensory integration is not working properly, it may take time before the person pulls back from a hot stove. Or she or he may reach for an object but miss as the arm goes awry. There is also something called the proprioception system, which is the muscles, joints, and tendons that provide a person with a subconscious understanding or feeling of where their body is within a space. You don't think of it but as you walk through a doorway, you can tell if you are going to make it thorough or walk into the door jam. For those with ASD, this ability may be compromised. Imagine not being able to tell how close you are to someone. This would make it impossible to find a space that works for you and the person you are speaking with.

In addition, there may be factors in the vestibular system that compromise those with ASD. *Vestibular* refers to balance and movement. Standing too near a person with ASD may create anxiety for that individual because he or she may believe the other person is going to come crashing into them.

A major aspect of social functioning for children is play. In fact, most of the norms in society, the development of appropriate social skills and other important aspects of child development, occur through play. Given the social issues with those with ASD it is a logical assumption that a child with ASD will have difficulty with play.

Concepts like imaginary play are an important stage in child development. Play can be considered a child's full-time job. Through play children learn problem solving, develop emotional responses, and develop empathy. Play helps children

Case Study 2

R is a seventeen-year-old girl with ASD. She is unable to get on an escalator. It seems the movement of the stairs is too overwhelming to be comfortably navigated. In addition, staircases present their own challenges. She takes a step at a time, but needs to touch the top side and landing of each step before she moves. R clings to the handrail and often does not let go as her feet descend.

When speaking with an individual, R initially stands a few inches from the person with little regard for that space. Work with her has included telling her to take a step back until a more appropriate distance is reached. Over time she has learned to take that initial step back from someone as she enters a conversation. As for the stairs and escalators, work with a physical therapist has provided R with many exercises to increase awareness of her proprioception.

Overall, R's ability to perform motor movements is weak. It is hard for her to pick things up or point, raise her hand, and complete other fine motor tasks. Because of a lack of body awareness, going to the bathroom can also be difficult. She has frequent accidents as a result of poor awareness of her muscles and body. This requires her to maintain a very rigid bathroom schedule to avoid any problems.

In this case it is clear how the sensory input R receives leads to very typical ASD behaviors. In this case the difficulties R has are related to her motor skills. Walking, judging distances, and understanding her body needs are areas of difficulty.

practice for the routines of daily life (what child doesn't love to play school?). Most important is the development of symbolic play. This is when a child begins to use objects as other things, for example, blocks become a building, a sponge in the bathtub is a monster, and a whole host of other imaginary scenarios.

For children with ASD, this is often difficult. They do not always have the capability to imagine an object as anything other than the object. Pretend play requires perspective taking (imagining you are a princess or a lion) and acting

Stages of Play

Stage 1: Solitary Play

Solitary play is the first stage of play. From birth to the age of two, children are generally in this stage. Children find items and toys that they manipulate and play with alone. They are very busy exploring and discovering their new world. These very young children tend to play alone regardless of whether other children are in the same room.

Stage 2: Parallel Play

The second stage of play begins around the age of two. Children play next to each other but engage in separate activities. They play side-by-side and watch and listen to each other. At this age they are interested in similar toys, yet each child plays on his or her own. It is the beginning of an awareness that others have similar interests and engage in play. Awareness of others is the first step in extending egocentric play to include others.

Stage 3: Associative Play

At this third stage most children are still playing independently but will imitate the actions of other children. For example, if one child stacks blocks to make a tower, a second child may do the same thing. The children begin to interact through talking, borrowing, and taking turns with toys, but each child acts alone.

Stage 4: Cooperative Play

This stage becomes quite apparent in the later preschool years (during the fourth and fifth years), when children have acquired the skills to interact together for the purpose of play. Speaking and listening skills are more developed so children can communicate with each other. Children can share ideas and tell each other what to do. Communication about play is the critical skill of cooperative play.[b]

through the character and characteristics of another. This is not something that comes easily for many children with ASD. (This will be discussed in later chapters.) Most young children with ASD do not seek to play with other children. Rather, they engage in solitary play. They often isolate themselves within the classroom and use objects in ways they were not intended. For example, a student with ASD may spin pencils or crayons over and over. Blocks get held and moved within the individual's gaze in a figure eight movement. A very common occurrence is the lining up of objects. Toy cars or figures are arranged in linear fashion over and over. It seems that many of these toys are used less for play and more for a visual or sensory stimulation (more will be discussed on this in chapter 5).

Restricted Patterns of Behavior

Along with social difficulties, many individuals with ASD display certain patterns of behavior that are repeated over and over, sometimes occupying great amounts of time. This behavior can be movements, how objects are used, or even repetitive speech patterns. This looks very different for each individual with ASD, but some of the common stereotyped behavior includes hand flapping, rocking, spinning, and moving objects back and forth. These movements are called *stims*, which refers to the fact they are stimulating in some way.

Persistent motor movements are the subject of many studies. Some individuals with ASD hold their hands close to the side of their heads and move or wiggle their fingers. Another common behavior that many individuals with ASD engage in is head rocking with their gaze fixed upon a point. These motor movements may last for seconds or hours, depending on the individual. These movements are compulsive and difficult to extinguish in the moment. Similar behavior is seen in another neurological disorder called Tourette's syndrome. This is a condition where an individual has a sudden, rapid, recurrent nonrhythmic motor movement or vocalization. This can be raising one's arm, shaking of the hands, making a repeated sound, or a host of other movements. Most people with this syndrome do not have cognitive impairments and can express their compulsions and explain why they have the need to move.

The difference between Tourette's tics and motor movements for individuals with ASD is that in Tourette's, tics are momentary and do not generally repeat immediately (in most cases) once the urge has been satisfied. With ASD the hand flapping can continue for an indefinite amount of time.

What do you do when your leg falls asleep? You stand, shake, and move. Perhaps with ASD there is that lack of sensory input, as we discussed, that leads to the repetition of behavior to satisfy that lack of sensory input. This means that a repetitive behavior is satisfying some sort of sensation need. Sensory dysfunction

Tourette's Syndrome: What Is a Tic?

Many individuals report a sensory basis for their tics. They feel the need to tic building up as a kind of tension in a particular anatomical location, and they feel that they consciously choose to release it. The sensations and internal events leading up to the expression of the tic are often referred to in the literature as "premonitory sensory phenomena," "urges," or by some other term. These urges or internal sensations or perceptions that something is "not just right" precede tics and compulsive behavior. Some research has reported that over 90 percent of people monitor urges prior to motor tics, with participants reporting that their most common sensation was an urge to move and an impulse to tic ("had to do it").

Tics can sometimes be suppressed, but most people's experience is that the tics will eventually be released. Thus, if you were to ask someone not to tic, you might observe that they could suppress a tic for a while, but eventually, they would have to release it.

What happens if the individual tries to suppress the tics? Some individuals have no control at all over their tics, while others have varying degrees of control. Most adults report that their ability to modify or suppress their tics improved as they matured, and recent research supports the notion that as the child matures, her or his awareness of the tics and the ability to suppress them increase.[c]

in ASD might lead to problems moving information that comes through the senses to the brain. People with ASD may have a lowered (hypoactive) sensory system or a heightened (hyperactive) one. Stims, like hand flapping, may work to help balance the senses. A person with a hypoactive sensory system may not receive enough input, and behavior like flapping can provide the input the person needs. A person with a hyperactive sensory system may engage in flapping to pull attention away from sensory overload.

Some people on the spectrum refer to self-stimulatory behavior as "self-regulating" behavior because the repetitive movements provide relief. Some of this self-stimulating behavior may be undetectable (like finger tapping or shifting in a chair); some may be very noticeable (like hand flapping or irregular body

Visual Symptoms and Individuals with ASD

● Visual symptoms highly associated with ASD

- Gaze aversion
- Turning head, looking out of corner of eye
- Being attracted to shiny surfaces or mirrors
- Prolonged fixating on light patterns, windows, or blinds
- Hyperfixating on one object while ignoring other objects in the room
- Always preferring/avoiding a particular color
- Showing distorted body postures or orientation including arching back, hyperextension of neck
- Toe walking
- Touching all surfaces (walls, furniture, etc.) when in an unfamiliar environment
- Anxiety or avoidance associated with fast moving objects or animals
- Spinning objects close to face
- Intense light sensitivity
- Poor attention to one's surroundings as well as a lack of interest in one's environment
- Preference for looking at objects (or parts of objects) rather than people

Visual symptoms included in the screening/diagnosis of ASD

- Poor eye contact
- Excessive lining up of toys or other objects
- Fidgeting with objects repetitively
- Maintaining interest in spinning objects for periods greater than a couple of minutes
- Not following where someone else is looking
- Walking on tiptoe
- Flicking fingers or hands near face
- Staring at nothing with no apparent purpose
- Excessive interest limited to a single toy[d]

movements). Strategies to reduce flapping and other motor stimulation require planning and self-monitoring procedures or reinforcement, and they may take a while to achieve results.[10]

Another interesting hypothesis regarding hand movements is that for those with ASD, peripheral vision might be compromised. It may be that a person's peripheral vision "falls asleep," which is why wiggling the fingers on the side of the head would stimulate and "wake up" peripheral vision processing. Another theory posits that when an individual processes too much visual information, he or she needs to create the stim in order to focus on one visual stimuli and not feel overwhelmed by too much visual processing.

The repetition of behavior goes beyond physical and can also be verbal. There are a few types of repetitive verbal behavior that are common in individuals with ASD. The first is echolalia. With echolalia, an individual repeats what is said. Thus, if you asked the question "How are you?" the individual repeats, "How are you?" rather than answer the question. The person may do so once, or repeat it over and over. Sometimes an individual will repeat what he hears in daily life. For example, I have heard many individuals with ASD repeat the announcements of the New York City subway conductor. You might hear "Please stand clear of the closing doors" or a list of the stops. Other students will repeat lines from television shows.

Idiosyncratic speech is another common feature of ASD. This is when the speech or language is used in unusual ways or in ways not relevant to the conversation. Sometimes it can be that echolalia phrases are brought into a conversation, or it can be that the person seems stuck on a phrase, for example, making a statement unrelated to the question "Do you have your homework?" by answering with "Today is windy." Many students have phrases they like to repeat. "Today is windy" comes from personal experience with a young woman who answered almost all questions with this phrase. At times this speech can be directed toward others; other times it is directed toward the individual. It is not uncommon to see individuals with ASD repeating phrases and terms to themselves.

Sameness

All people like to know what to expect during the day. Surprises are nice, but when you go to class, you like to know what to expect. You know who the teacher is, who you sit next to, and what the topic will be. For those with ASD, sameness is something that seems to be a necessary element for their daily functioning. People with ASD can hold to a very rigid and inflexible schedule throughout the day. If lunch is at 12:15, 12:16 lunch will create great tension, stress, and even anger. For some little changes make a big difference. Many students insist on

Case Study 3

E is a twelve-year-old student who was diagnosed with ASD. His behavior includes repetitive verbal phrases and motor movements. When walking from one class to another, E will almost always engage in self-talk where he repeats the closing credits from a public television show. His verbal language in general is limited to one- or two-word phrases. However, when engaged in self-talk he will recite several continuous sentences from the broadcast: "This program was brought to you today by a generous grant from the . . . " and goes on to describe the rest of the narration. When asked a question such as "E, have you eaten your lunch?" he will repeat the question back.

E's motor behavior is also repetitive and pervasive throughout the day. With palms flat facing his eyes, he moves his hands together and apart in an open and closed fashion. He also waves his hands next to his eyes. Generally, his gaze is fixed on the floor, and he does not make eye contact with the person who engages him. When motor movements are disrupted (by a teacher or peer), E becomes upset and screams.

Additionally, E often pulls threads from his clothing and spins them between his fingers. He can be consumed by this for upwards of thirty minutes. He also pulls thin strips of paper, leaves, and twigs and uses them in the same way.

wearing one particular article of clothing all the time. There are many individuals with ASD who will only eat certain foods. One student in particular who comes to mind ate a veggie hot dog every day for five years. To my knowledge, she is still only having a hot dog for lunch.

Sameness for certain items is common and so is sameness for certain routines. School schedules are most noticeable. If the schedule changes, some students have a very difficult time making the change. Some might complain mildly but others will repeat over and over that "this is not where we are supposed to be." Often a change in schedule will result in tantrums and great anxiety. For those with ASD, routines and schedules are important as their flexibility is compromised. In addition, many with ASD who are overloaded with sensory information may rely on the sameness of routines to navigate the day. Any change results in a collapse of their understanding of how to deal with moving from one thing to the next. Many classrooms for students with ASD have printed schedules for the day that the student holds on to all day so there are no surprises.

In a large city, public transportation is the general mode of moving from place to place. Students with ASD often have a fixation or fascination with the subway system. For students who can independently travel, any service change or delay can create a problem. I have known students who have walked home (several miles) when a certain train was not in operation, even though another train would have taken them to the same location. For example, the number 1 train and the number 2 train both stop at Ninety-Sixth Street. But for one young man, taking the number 2 train to Ninety-Sixth Street was out of the question. He would only take the number 1 train. On a day when the number 1 train was not running, he walked home. When asked why he walked home (knowing full well the 2 would have gotten him there), he replied, "I take the 1 train." That's it. No other explanation needed. The 1 train is what he does, not the 2 train. Many parents have commented that when driving home, they must take the same route. Regardless of traffic, when they veer off course, the child breaks into a tantrum.

Sameness can apply to thinking. Rigid patterns of thinking are often associated with ASD. How to do something must follow a certain script. For example, writing can be difficult for some students with ASD. Not because of the writing itself, but because if the letter does not look perfect, the student will erase and begin again, over and over. It becomes almost impossible for some to finish a sentence. During a home economics class, a student would wash and dry one plate, then put it away before going on to the next dish. When told he could wash the dish and let it dry on the rack without having to turn the water on and off, his response was, "This is how I do it."

Rigid Interests

You have read about the issues of social conversation with individuals with ASD. Some of this stems from the rigid interests individuals with ASD may have. For many individuals, topics of interest and conversation are very limited. Things like transportation, movies, cartoon characters, and so on all create what we would refer to as a specialty interest. A specialty interest is a topic the individual with ASD becomes an expert about. Some students may know everything there is to know about a topic; however, the knowledge base is factual and usually limited to one or two categories. Interests in transportation are common, especially in different transportation categories. Individuals with ASD may know everything about different types of airplanes or cars. The student who would not take the number 2 train knew everything there was to know about the subways of New York. He could tell you every stop on every train (that's about five hundred stations) and could give you directions via the subway. But of course, he could not take the 2 train. Thus, this knowledge is concrete and factual rather than procedural.

These interests may often be obsessions, or very rigid in nature. For example, a student who has an interest in *Star Wars* may be unable to talk about anything else in a conversation. This is obviously limiting in one's ability to develop interpersonal relationships. If the first question you ask is, "Do you like *Star Wars*," and the response is no, what next? You or I could move on to another topic. For those with ASD, it is not that easy. The rigidity in the interest limits the ability to move on to the next topic. Like a broken record (if you know what that is!), the topic is the same over and over and over. Many parents complain about the intensity with which the interest is explored. For some individuals if it isn't *Star Wars*, it is irrelevant.

Many individuals with ASD seem to develop interests in categorical data such as the order of the presidents of the United States, state capitals, Oscar-winning movies, and other topics where a list may be generated. Later on you will read about special talents of some people with ASD, and strong memory skills for certain facts seems to be a catalyst for these specialty interests.

Pokémon is a popular television series, game, and website that has captured much attention in the popular culture. If you look online, you will see there is much written about the connection between Pokémon and ASD. For many children and young adults with ASD, Pokémon is a favorite. Each character in this world has very specific characteristics unique to the specific creature. Perhaps the specificity of the characters and the organizational structure fits within the necessary features a special interest must have. Another favorite of young children is Thomas the Train. While these cartoon worlds are enjoyed by many children for a number of years, the interest for ASD students seems to last longer than for most children. While most students grow out of their Pokémon or Thomas interest, those with ASD may maintain these interests throughout high school.

These types of special interests may be socially appropriate in the early years. However, there are some special interests an individual may have that do not lend themselves to socially appropriate situations. Some individuals have an intense interest in appliances like copy machines and microwaves, or in the opening and closing of doors. These interests may be satisfying a sensory issue (like the movement of opening and closing of a door). For others it may be the expectation of paper coming from a copy machine. One high school student I met years ago knew the name of every printer and the ink cartridge type it needed. These are special interests that don't necessarily fit into the daily conversations people have. Problems may arise when the situation does not allow for the individual to explore the interest. One parent I worked with reported that her eleven-year-old son climbed over the partition at the motor vehicle office to get a look at the copy machine. This interest to see the machine certainly caused some trouble.

In general, special interests seem to fit into two categories. The first is categorical information such as types of transportation or names of presidents. The other seems to be those things that provide a sensory experience, like the visual movement of a fan or the whirring of the refrigerator motor.

Phobias

Special interests can have a downside. Many individuals with ASD have fears of special objects. Balloons, for example, are something I have repeatedly seen children with ASD run from. The fear may be from the anticipation of the noise it makes when it pops.[11] Many fears center on animals, for example, dogs, birds, and squirrels, as I have witnessed firsthand. Again, the fear seems more anticipatory in that the fear is not the animal as much as the animal jumping on the individual. The intense focus on these items can be debilitating. I worked with an individual afraid of bees. He refused to leave the building every day as he thought there would be bees outside.

Some research has pointed to the fact that those with ASD do have more fears than other groups. But these fears were generally situational or the fear of an object or specific thing. Individuals with ASD were not reported to have a higher fear of injury or harm than any other group. Because anxiety is a common feature with ASD, it seems that the phobias that individuals face can be daunting and lifelong.

Sensitivity

Imagine wearing a set of clothing made out of sandpaper. Everything! Shirt, pants, socks, and underwear. How long would you last? Well then imagine your tolerance for fabric was dropped to the point that a cotton shirt felt like sandpaper. You would feel every fiber as it moved on your body. That may be the case for some individuals with ASD. As in all cases, there are levels of tolerance, but there are those for whom clothing is painful. Or what if you put headphones on and blasted Metallica at the highest volume? It would probably hurt your ears. On the other hand, imagine if you could not feel that hot stove? Or discriminate when someone was talking to you as opposed to other conversations going on in the room. More about sensory issues is included in chapter 5, but know that over- and undersensitivity toward sight, touch, taste, sound, and smell can all be major

Most Unusual Fears

● The most frequently reported categories of unusual fears include the following:

- Mechanical things (blenders, can openers, cassette players, ceiling fans, clothes dryers, drills, electric toothbrushes, exhaust fans, hair dryers, hand dryers, leaf blowers, toilets, vacuum cleaners, washing machines, water fountains, wheelchairs, windshield wipers)
- Heights (elevators, escalators, heights, steps)
- Weather (cloudy weather, rain, thunderstorms, wind, natural disasters such as floods, droughts, hurricanes, and tornadoes)
- Nonmechanical things (balloons, black television screens, buttons, clamshells, crayons, dolls, drains, electrical outlets, eyes on toys, garden hoses, glass tabletops, glow-in-the-dark stars, gum under table, hair in bathtub, lights, mole on person's face, moon, shadows, strings, stuffed animals, swinging or rocking things, tall things, things on ceiling, vents on house)
- Places (bathrooms, bedrooms, certain houses or restaurants, closed or small spaces, garages, large or open spaces, rooms with doors unlocked or open)
- Worries about dying (bone breaking through chest, car accident, drowning, eaten by fleas, heart attack, murdered, natural disaster, poisoned, spleen exploding, world ending, germs or contamination, running out of certain foods)
- Visual media (characters in or segments of movies, television shows, commercials, computer games)[e]

issues for those with ASD. If you look at the seven senses (yes, seven; not five) sight, touch, hearing, taste, smell, proprioception (body awareness), and vestibular (balance), for individuals with ASD, there are repeated patterns of difficulty maintaining a level of comfort that you or I might not experience.

Many people with ASD can experience difficulties with either being acutely or not sensitive to these seven senses. For some, a faint smell may be too much to handle. Think about a classroom with ten or twelve students playing. The noise might be overwhelming for some students, to the extent they are in discomfort.

Many years ago florescent lights would flicker at sixty times per minute. This was not detectable for most, but those with hypersensitive visual processing would see every flicker. It would be like watching a movie on film and seeing every frame blur from one to the next. These days, fluorescent lights flicker at about forty thousand times per minute so it is not a problem anymore. In any case, it is clear that sensitivity levels for sensory experiences may be different for those with ASD compared to the general population.

Summing Up

While all of these features of ASD are common, they by no means explain everything. ASD includes the word *spectrum*. Any spectrum can go from very little to very large. So for ASD any of the topics we discuss can go from not really an issue to a big issue. Every person is different and will display different behavior.

For someone to receive a diagnosis of ASD, these symptoms or traits must be observable at a young age. ASD is not something that appears in later years, old age, teenage years, or adulthood. It is evident generally from birth and diagnosed in the first few years of life.

Another essential point when diagnosing ASD is that these impairments must interfere with social, job, or life functioning. Personally, I don't like wool sweaters. They make me itch. But I can still work or carry on with my daily tasks in a wool sweater (I just won't wear them). My sensitivity to wool sweaters doesn't interfere with my life or the things I have to do during a typical day. Even with some difficulties many people with ASD live a life like you or me, but they may have to make some compromises. For example, they may need help on the job to make sure they are carrying out the tasks assigned to them. In other cases, they may need a social worker to come to their homes to make sure bills are paid, medical appointments are made, and the upkeep of the home is acceptable. Always remember the term *spectrum* because the variability from one person to the next is very big.

Finally, when we are determining a diagnosis of ASD we need to make sure there is nothing else that might better explain a person's needs. For example, traumatic brain injury can result in behavior similar to that seen in ASD. So can obsessive compulsive disorder. In addition, cognitive deficits found in those with intellectual disabilities may occur together. But these diagnoses may require different treatment even when there is behavior similar to that seen in ASD.

3

WHAT'S IN A NAME?
A HISTORICAL
LOOK AT ASD

Autism. When you say the word, it is a natural part of our modern-day vocabulary. It is associated with movies, media, and the subject of many books. People automatically think of the movie *Rain Man* or think of a person with mind-boggling skills in math or music. In today's world it would seem that everyone knows a person with autism (some studies say one out of fifty-five people). So today, the word *autism* is well embedded in our vocabulary. But where did the word come from? It has been around for a while and its meaning has changed over time. The way we use the word today is much different than when it was originally coined.

Paul Eugen Bleuler, MD

The word *autism* comes from Paul Eugen Bleuler, born in 1857 in Zurich. One of the most influential psychologists and psychiatrists of the nineteenth century, he was a contemporary of Sigmund Freud. Bleuler spent his time working and studying people with schizophrenia, a condition that exists, usually in adults, where the lines between reality and fantasy become blurred. Many individuals hear voices or see things that are not there. It was Bleuler who gave the name schizophrenia to this condition after working with his patients. Initially, his patients were referred to as patients with dementia. But with close observation, Bleuler came to the realization that their condition included a splitting of thoughts often involving contradictory attitudes or ideas. Thus, he referred to them as people with schizophrenia, a term whose Greek roots actually mean "a splitting of the mind."

There were other symptoms of schizophrenia that Bleuler noticed were common among his patients. Patients seemed to be very self-involved and focused

Dr. Paul Eugene Bleuler

Paul Eugene Bleuler (1857–1939) used the word *autism* to describe a symptom of schizophrenia. His work with individuals with schizophrenia led him to categorize behavior. He saw that his unique patients had behavior he termed the 4 As:

- Affect—inappropriate or flattened emotions usually not matching the situation
- Autism—social withdrawal, living in a fantasy world
- Ambivalence—conflicting attitudes of the self and others
- Associations—loosening of thoughts, randomization of ideas[a]

inward to a world of their own. To this symptom he applied the Greek root *autos*, meaning "the self," and coined the term *autism*.

In 1911 we have our first record of the word. Bleuler used the term *autism* to refer to a specific symptom of schizophrenia, not a unique condition. It would be more than thirty years later, in 1943, before autism was diagnosed as a condition unto itself.

Leo Kanner, MD

Leo Kanner was a pioneer in child psychiatry at the time Blueler was working with schizophrenia. Born in Austria and schooled in Berlin, Kanner came to the United States in 1930 and founded the first center for child psychiatry in Baltimore at Johns Hopkins University. In 1935 he wrote *Child Psychiatry*, the first English-language book on the topic.

Kanner had received a thirty-three-page letter from the father of a boy named Donald. The letter described, in detail, the unusual behavior of the five-year-old boy. The letter described behavior such as obsessive spinning of objects, a preference to be alone, a tendency to ignore everything around him, spinning himself in circles, and rocking his head from side to side. It also described how Donald would repeat words and phrases over and over. In addition, Donald would break into explosive tantrums every time his routine was disrupted.[1]

Donald's family visited Dr. Kanner, travelling from Mississippi to Baltimore. While working with Donald, Kanner began to recognize traits that were similar to other children he worked with. For perhaps the first time, the realization came

Dr. Leo Kanner

Dr. Leo Kanner (1894–1981) was the first person to give a diagnosis of autism. Dr. Kanner's work with children set the stage for years of research to follow. In his 1943 paper "Autistic Disturbances of Affective Contact," he reported on repetitive behavior, a turn inward into one's own world, difficulty with relationships, and echolalia (repeating words and phrases over and over) as common characteristics of his young patients. He stated in his paper that the parents of the children he worked with lacked warmth and emotion. This was something his predecessors focused on when developing a theory of why autism occurred in these children. This statement ignited the spark that led future researchers (such as Bruno Bettelheim) to develop their theories.[b]

that a unique condition existed among these children. As Kanner described it, these children had a need for aloneness and sameness, and they displayed a variety of behavioral conditions. All the children were physically typical, although some of them reportedly had large heads. Another common element: all the children were prone to extreme tantrums. In his paper "Autistic Disturbances of Affective Contact," Kanner, for the first time, diagnosed the condition of autism. His paper concluded that these children came into the world with an inability for social contact or emotional reciprocity.

Donald T.

Donald T., the first person to be diagnosed with autism, was born in 1938. After his parents noticed behavior that was unusual, they met with Dr. Kanner, who diagnosed a new syndrome, autism. Donald was born and raised in the small town of Forest, Mississippi. He grew up to be a respected member of his community and worked as a teller at a local bank. Donald attended community college and developed an interest in golf. Friends and family talked of his amazing ability to remember his golf score on any given day he had played. Donald is a world traveler having visited thirty-six countries and many parts of the United States. In 2014 he turned eighty-two years old and lives on his own in the house he grew up in with his family.[c]

Dr. Kanner also concluded that all eleven children in his study had come from highly intelligent families. Five of the fathers were psychiatrists. There were lawyers, doctors, writers, as well. Nine of the eleven mothers were college graduates. An important comment in his paper was that very few of the parents were warmhearted. He reported that most were more involved in scientific, artistic, or literary interests and had little interest in other people. Why is this important to mention? As we look at early thinking about the causes of autism, it will become abundantly clear.

Hans Asperger, MD

About the same time Leo Kanner was developing his theories, another important psychiatrist, Hans Asperger, was working with a similar population of children. Asperger was born in Vienna in 1906. While he and Kanner never met, their work led them to similar conclusions. Asperger, who had worked with hundreds of children, wrote a paper in 1944 called "Autistic Psychopaths in Childhood," based on four boys he had worked with. He noted that the boys had difficulty making social relationships, did not display empathy, had one-sided conversations, and had compulsive special interests. Asperger called these boys "little professors" due to the fact that they could talk in great detail about their favorite interests.[2] Interestingly, Hans Asperger had displayed several of these tendencies himself as a young man. Described as a "loner," Asperger had difficulty making friends. He was consumed with poetry, which he would recite to others (whether or not they wanted to hear it). Asperger was also known to refer to himself in the third person and quote himself.[3]

Two important distinctions are to be made between Kanner and Asperger. First, Asperger believed that these children with autistic behavior would use their special interests to further themselves in life. For example, one of his students went on to become an important scientist and mathematician. Whereas

---

Dr. Hans Asperger

Hans Asperger (1906–1980) worked with many students who had no seemingly cognitive deficits or language delays but did have difficulty with social interactions and maintaining social boundaries. To this form of autism the term *Asperger's syndrome* was given, a form of autism that was considered less severe. Until 2015 this term was used. Hans Asperger died in 1980. His birthday, February 18, is still regarded as International Asperger's Day.[d]

Kanner focused on the deficits, Asperger was keen on understanding the children's special talents. Second, Asperger realized that these symptoms were on a continuum, or spectrum. He understood that the severity of symptoms varied among children.

In the mid-1940s Asperger opened a school in Germany for students with autistic behavior. However, with World War II still happening, the school was destroyed in a bombing raid by the allied forces. Many of Asperger's early papers and work were lost. The articles and papers that did survive were written in German and were not noticed by the rest of the world. When Asperger's work was translated, Dr. Lorna Wing, a psychiatrist from England, recognized its importance. In 1981 she introduced the term *Asperger's syndrome*.[4] This diagnosis was given to children who displayed autistic behavior without language or learning deficits. Most notably, they had deficits in social functioning. In the 1980s children diagnosed with Asperger's syndrome were also referred to as "high-functioning autistic" children, a term that has fallen out of favor.

Autism, Why? Says Who?

To really understand the early theories of what caused autism, you have to understand the psychological thinking of the time. Remember that psychology is the study of behavior. Thus, if we think of the early days of psychology in this country, psychologists relied on what they could directly observe and see with their own eyes. Brain scans or imaging would not come for many years. Thus, the leading psychological thinking of the time was referred to as behaviorism.

Behaviorism is basically the theory that when individuals engage in specific behavior, they are either rewarded for it or punished. Obviously, if one is rewarded, she or he is more likely to engage in that behavior again. When punished, well, we all know what happens. After you touch a hot stove, you probably won't do it again. This applies to animals and people alike. Even babies' behavior is the result of rewards. For example, when a baby babbles, parents generally respond with baby talk. The baby gets attention, which is a reward, and the baby will engage in that behavior more frequently. The babies are conditioned to babble as a result of the positive reinforcement of their parents.

At this point it was clear that autism was a unique condition. It was not simply a subset of behavior related to schizophrenia or another syndrome. The new definition of autism quickly gained acceptance. So as this condition gained attention, the next logical question was why it occurred in the first place. Was this a disorder present at birth? Or was it something that occurred in the early months or years of life? This debate lasted a while before anything definitive could be discovered.

John Watson, PhD

Like any theory, behaviorism was subject to many tests in the early part of the twentieth century. One famous (but relatively cruel) experiment referred to as "Little Albert" was conducted by John Watson. Watson believed that he could "train" or condition people's emotions as well as their behavior. Watson was so firm in his beliefs that he believed he could take any infant in the world and train him to grow up to be whatever Watson chose. He famously wrote a book called *Behaviorism* in 1924 that influenced thinking for many years. In his book Watson wrote,

> Give me a dozen healthy infants, well-formed, and my own specified world to bring them up in and I'll guarantee to take any one at random and train him to become any type of specialist I might select—doctor, lawyer, artist, merchant-chief, and, yes, even beggar man and thief, regardless of his talents, penchants, tendencies, abilities, vocations, and race of his ancestors. I am going beyond my facts and I admit it, but so have the advocates of the contrary and they have been doing it for many thousands of years.[5]

Watson, like all behaviorists, believed that the environment was solely responsible for the behavior in which we engage. Poor Little Albert was the subject of Watson trying to prove this. Watson presented the toddler with a small white rat. At the same time an assistant produced a loud banging sound behind Albert, loud enough to startle the child. Once the banging started, Little Albert burst into tears. This was done repeatedly with Albert crying every time. Eventually, the white rat was presented without the banging, yet Little Albert still cried and tried to get away; thus, Watson believed he had conditioned the child to fear white rats. Albert had associated the white rat with the banging. His crying with the presentation of the rat alone was proof. Watson never followed up to see if Albert remained afraid of rats after this study. This was a major criticism other researchers have cited.

Little Albert Experiment

Fortunately, toddlers are no longer subject to experiments that cause emotional harm. Scaring Little Albert in this experiment would never be allowed today. Sadly, Little Albert died a few years after the experiment due to acquired hydrocephalus. No one ever knew if his conditioned fear of rats persisted after this experiment.

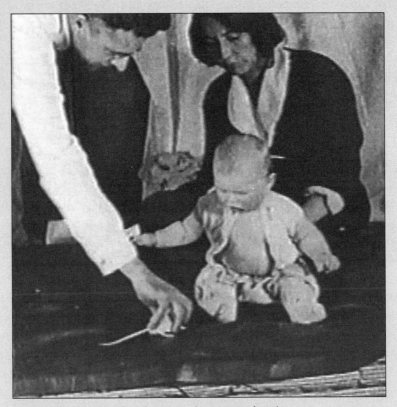

Little Albert waits for the experiments to begin.

Since then, laws and ethics have advanced to protect research participants. There are strict guidelines about research that declare no harm be done to the individual, nor should there be any infliction of pain. John Watson is perhaps an extreme example of the thinking of the time.[e]

Sigmund Freud

The early twentieth century was revolutionary for the study of psychology. Adding to the prominent thinking of the time was none other than Sigmund Freud (1856–1939). Freud's name is almost synonymous with psychology and he was extremely influential in the medical field as well. His work on early child development, dream interpretation, and ego development all set the stage for a psychodynamic theory of human development. Psychodynamic means that one's conscious and subconscious minds are what controls and regulates behavior. Things can happen to us at an early age that we cannot remember, but our subconscious might hold onto these memories, which in turn can influence our behavior. Freud proposed that psychological disorders of the human mind were not caused by organic factors in the brain but rather by an early childhood trauma. Negative childhood experiences were the basis for unhealthy development in the human mind.

Now that we know a little about Watson, Freud, and the thinking of the time, let's go back to Leo Kanner's study. He said two interesting things that would set the stage for what would become a well-accepted theory of how autism developed. First he said that the students were "probably" born with an innate structure that influenced the behavior of autism. He also stated that the parents of the children were not warmhearted. Scientists of the time paid close attention to Dr. Kanner's paper. One of those scientists was Bruno Bettelheim, an influential professor. He studied Kanner's words and would soon shape popular thinking around autism.

Bruno Bettelheim, Psychologist

Bettelheim (1903–1990) was born in Austria and came to America in 1939 upon his liberation from a German concentration camp and began his tenure as a psychology professor at the University of Chicago. During his time at the university, he worked with children and developed his theory of why autism had occurred within the individual. During this time the ideas of Watson and Freud were well accepted. He also used Kanner's idea that parents of children with autism were not warmhearted to help form his theories. With this in mind, Bettelheim stated that autism was an emotional disorder that developed in some children because of psychological harm brought upon them by their mothers.[6] The conditions of early childhood would influence the development of the child. In 1950, Bettelheim coined the term *refrigerator mothers*. It was a term to explain the formation of autism in the child. Because of the cold and distant relationship the mother had with her child, the child would turn inward as there was no reinforcement of attention or care. It was the mother's indifferent treatment, Bettelheim thought, that caused autism. Bettelheim also drew on his experiences in the concentration camp and compared them to autism. He stated that being trapped in one's mind was similar to being trapped in a concentration camp. That is a very powerful statement. Bettelheim's ideas were pretty dismal and accusatory.

His theory spread quickly thanks to the advent of television. In 1954, the first color broadcast was aired across the country. Television reached millions of viewers and could spread information faster than ever. Bettelheim used this medium to share his findings. Across many television shows, radio broadcasts, and magazines, Bettelheim's concept of the refrigerator mothers would become the most accepted cause of autism, influencing the medical and psychological worlds. In 1967 he released his book *The Empty Fortress: Infantile Autism and the Birth of the Self*, which was well read by the country. Bettelheim continued to promote his books and ideas nationwide.

Imagine for a second finding out that you, as a mother, were responsible for your child's autism. Today we can discount this idea, but at the time it was devastating for thousands. Mothers who doted over their children and who were model parents doing a wonderful job were blamed. It would be another twenty-five years before Bettelheim's theory of autism was challenged.

There are many reasons that the concept of refrigerator mothers is simply not true and has since been debunked because of social pressures and lack of scientific research. First let's look at some issues with Kanner's study that Bettelheim used to develop his theory. He relied on Kanner's statement that the parents of children with autism were not warmhearted and were distant. This impressed Bettelheim.

Bruno Bettelheim

Bettelheim was also fascinated with fairy tales and fantasy. He wrote books on the emotional and symbolic importance of fairy tales for children. He believed the themes would help students develop meaning and purpose in their lives. By relating to these stories, students could better prepare for their future. Bettelheim suggested that traditional fairy tales, with themes of abandonment, death, and injuries, allowed children to explore with their fears in symbolic terms. When children read these fairy tales, they could interpret them in their own ways. Bettelheim thought that by using these universally appealing stories, students could go through appropriate emotional growth. In the United States, Bettelheim won two major awards for *The Uses of Enchantment*: the National Book Critics Circle Award for Criticism and the National Book Award in the category of Contemporary Thought.[f]

But, there were only eleven children in Kanner's study. We know today that this group of children is too small a sample to make any conclusions about anything. A large sample is always required to draw conclusions about a population. In her book *The Autistic Brain* (2014), Temple Grandin makes the argument that while Kanner believed the parent's lack of warmth led to autism, it was more likely that the autism led to the lack of warmth or warmheartedness.[7] Children with autism are generally withdrawn or have a lack of social interaction with people. It seems obvious that an emotional distance would be caused as a result of the child not being able to reciprocate warmth, affection, or communication. Thus, parents would certainly react to the lack of response from their children by holding back. If a child screams every time a parent gives him or her a hug, the parent probably won't be hugging the child. In essence, Bettelheim's basis for refrigerator mothers was flawed from the beginning. He took information from Kanner's study without thinking it through or testing the hypothesis for himself.

After Bettelheim passed away in 1990, he was the subject of a controversial book in 1997. Richard Pollak, a journalist, was the brother of a boy with autism. When Pollak's brother died in an accident, Pollak decided to visit the Orthogenic School established by Bettelheim in Chicago that his brother had attended as a child.

Bettelheim had set up this school to work with children with autism. Pollak's hope was to gain a better understanding of his brother by visiting the school and speaking with Bettelheim. Their conversation was less than insightful. Bettelheim declared that Pollak's father was "simple-minded" and his mother rejected his brother at birth. Therefore, his brother committed suicide and was not the victim of an accident. These responses were not what Pollak expected. Bettelheim's words were harsh and seemed a bit strange to Pollak. The accusations Bettelheim spouted prompted Pollak to dig into the life of the psychologist. After meeting with several of Bettelheim's children, his ex-wife, and many colleagues, Pollak realized there were some inconsistencies in his life story. Pollak came away with the sense Bettelheim overstated his credentials and often exaggerated his findings. His backstory did not match the facts. Could it be that Bettelheim never even graduated from the University of Vienna, as he claimed? While the book is controversial, it does make us reflect on the weight that we put on scientific research and how easy it is to be misled. The twenty-five years of the refrigerator mother theory took its toll on many families.

Bernard Rimland, Psychologist

Bernard Rimland (1928–2006) was a research psychologist who worked around the same time Bettelheim was enjoying his success. In 1956, Rimland's wife gave

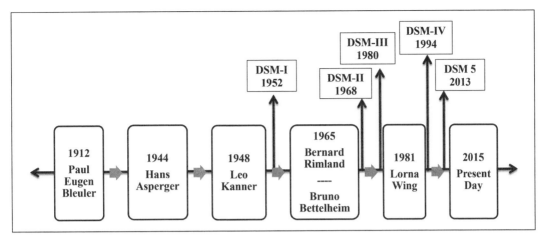

A timeline of thinking and important ASD milestones. Important to note is the interjection of the *Diagnostic and Statistical Manual of Mental Disorders* (*DSM*). The *DSM* is the book doctors and psychologists use to help diagnose various mental disorders. The publication of newer versions of the *DSM* was certainly influenced by the times. Different theories and different directions of popular thinking were part of the reasoning that went into diagnosing autism. *Courtesy of the author*

birth to a son with autism. From his firsthand experiences and research, Rimland questioned the theory that autism was the result of a distant parent-child relationship and presented the first argument that autism was a biological condition. Despite the publication of his book *Infantile Autism: The Syndrome and Its Implication for a Neural Theory of Behavior* (1964), Rimland didn't have the same media attention as did Bruno Bettelheim, so his work and theories went largely unnoticed by the public. But like any good idea, news of his work began to slowly spread. Parents gladly supported a theory that no longer blamed them for their children's autism. Rimland quickly gained support in the parent community and became recognized in the field of autism research. In addition, Rimland set up several important groups to support further research and parent support. Thanks to Rimland, the study of autism would now include scientific research. Even Dr. Kanner recognized the importance of Rimland's work and agreed that there was a biological cause to autism. Rimland got the attention he deserved and even went on to serve as a consultant on the movie *Rain Man* in 1988.

Andrew Wakefield, MD

You may have heard that at some point many people were convinced that autism was a result of the measles, mumps, rubella (MMR) vaccine. For a while it was all over the news. And even though studies had found no evidence whatsoever, people still believed that there was a relationship. So much so that the drop in the number of vaccinations in the United States produced the highest level of measles cases since the disease was seemingly eradicated. So why was this theory so popular that in 2014 a survey reported that a third of parents in this country believed autism was caused by vaccines?[8]

It all started with twelve children and one doctor. British surgeon Andrew Wakefield published a paper in 1998 that shocked many. He wrote that parents and doctors had reported that their children did not have any symptoms of autism until after they had been inoculated with MMR vaccine.[9] This sounds like a home run in coming up with a cause for autism. It was certainly embraced by the public. While few read the actual paper, the news of the study spread. It also should be noted that the paper never said that the MMR vaccine actually caused autism (and several other maladies). It simply reported the observations and opinions of parents and doctors.

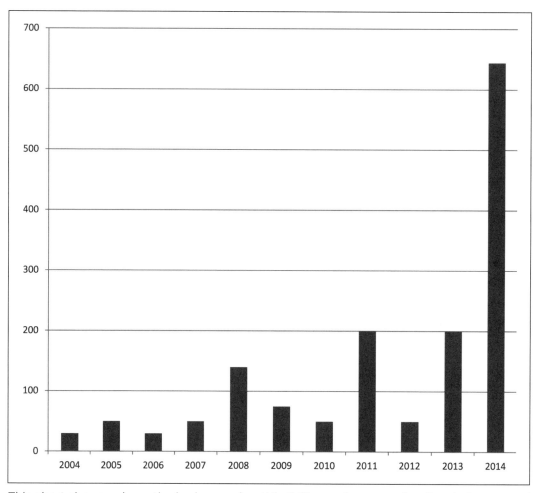

This chart shows a dramatic rise in measles. Why? The controversy of autism being caused by vaccines led to a decrease in vaccinations, which led to a rise in measles, a disease that had almost been eradicated in the United States. *From Centers for Disease Control,* Morbidity and Mortality Weekly Report *63, no. 22 (June 6, 2014)*

Lots of information came out about Andrew Wakefield's study over time. There were issues relating to fraudulent data and falsified statistics. Critics even stated that he was motivated to find a connection for financial reasons. He had a patent pending for a vaccine of his own, although he argued it was a nutritional supplement. Wakefield lost his license to practice medicine, and the journal that had published his paper retracted it entirely.[10]

Time and time again, study after study, researchers have found no relationship between autism and vaccines. This entire book could be a report of the many studies finding no connection between autism and vaccine. So why then do people still believe there is a correlation? Wakefield's paper was well publicized. Perhaps the damage had been done. No matter how many papers come out disproving a connection, people may always be skeptical.

If Not, Then What?

So far we can establish that the popular thinking shifted to an innate structure that seemed to be the key to understanding how autism occurs. But innate can mean lots of things. Could autism be a genetic thing? That is, could genes be damaged or changed in such a way that autism could occur? This is the case with syndromes like fragile X and Down syndrome. In both these cases changes in the gene structure cause a very specific change in the fetal development. There are more than five thousand diseases related to a single gene mutation.

Could autism be hereditary? Perhaps it is a genetic trait that is passed from one generation to another. Lots of traits are hereditary. In many cases a disease may not show up in an individual even when he or she carries the gene. Many recessive genes will not manifest unless an individual has the recessive trait from both parents. In some cases inheriting a gene from one parent gives the child a 50 percent chance of having the disease (like Huntington's disease). Then there is the concept of multifactorial cause. This is when one may carry a gene for a disease, such as cancer or heart disease, but the disease only occurs when environmental factors are added. For example, if one smoked and carried a gene related to cancer it would be referred to as a multifactorial cause that produced the cancer in the individual.

Genes and Autism

Girls and boys also change the odds of autism. It is clear that autism is less frequent in girls. But the sex of the first child with autism influences the chance that a second or third child will also have autism. A girl with autism is more likely to

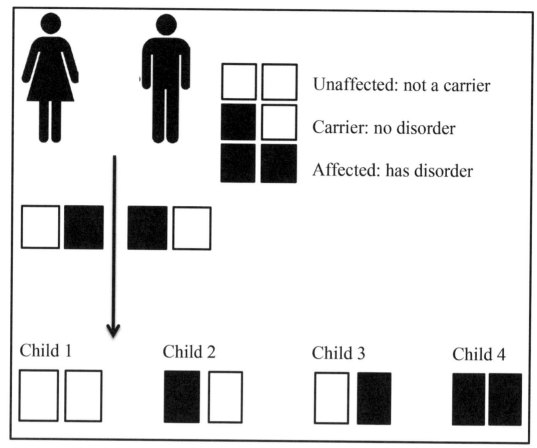

Both expressive and recessive genes exist within our human structure. Dominant, or expressive, genes will generally show up as characteristics. But recessive genes need a partner gene to express a trait. A dominant gene can produce an outcome without a partner. Recessive genes can be passed down from generation to generation without being expressed. They can only be expressive if they have another similar gene as a partner. An example is with eye color. A boy's parents can both have brown eyes while the boy himself has blue eyes. This shows that the parents are both carriers of the recessive gene for eye color, but they have a dominant gene as well. In many cases one may carry the two recessive genes for the disorder (like the child to the far right), but environmental factors are needed to trigger the effects. *Courtesy of the author*

have a sibling with autism than a boy. The risk factor for boys and girls goes down with each subsequent sibling.

Let's look at the relationship between siblings. If there is some correlation between siblings and autism, that might suggest some sort of heritable trait is passed on by the parents. Well, there were plenty of studies in the 1980s and 1990s that concluded that there was indeed a relationship. In a 2013 population study, Danish researchers found that a family with a child with autism has a 7 percent chance of having a second child with autism.[11] This might not seem high, but remember that of the entire population only 1.2 percent are identified with

Emma and Noa

Emma and Noa are sisters who have both been diagnosed with autism spectrum disorder. The two high school students share many qualities (as do most sisters) but are very different in other ways. Emma is a friendly high school student who loves the theater and is a gifted actress herself. She has been the lead in her high school play and will continue to participate in the musical theater of her high school. She enjoys singing as well. In the last play she had several solos and received standing ovations! Emma is not shy about hosting weekly assemblies as well. During her years in middle school she would often host and introduce students and teachers in their presentations. Emma says her favorite part of school is hanging out with her friends. She loves her teachers and all the subjects they teach. Emma has a busy life outside of school and attends many after-school art and music programs. Emma hopes to work as a teacher someday.

Meet Emma (left; age fourteen) and Noa (right; age seventeen), sisters who share some traits, but are also very different. *Courtesy of the author*

Noa is a gifted artist. She brings great life to her work. Her art is filled with characters expressing emotion and feeling. While self-expression is difficult for Noa, she has found her means of expression. Emma and Noa's mom, Maria, highlights the many ways in which they are different and alike:

Emma has a more diverse pallet and enjoys spicy food. Whenever possible, she'll put hot sauce on everything (takes after Dad), whereas Noa prefers simple-looking meals like pasta, pizza, white rice, and bread. Noa's favorite dish is baked chicken wings. Emma, on the other hand, does not like chicken wings. Noa has an average appetite, and Emma has a voracious appetite. However, both enjoy Abuela's octopus salad and frog legs at their favorite Vietnamese restaurant in China Town!

Noa loves to go to Lincoln Center for the ballet shows. Her favorites include *Giselle*, *Swan Lake*, *The Nutcracker*, and she wants to see *Cinderella*. She enjoys all types of music from pop to lounge and classical music. Her favorite pop group is from South Korea: Girls' Generation. Emma likes mainstream pop music and enjoys singing all the Disney Princess movie songs. Her favor pop artist is Miley Cyrus.

Noa is more quiet and reserved. She's very much an introvert, learning quietly and by observation at best. Whereas Emma is more outgoing and shows interest in engaging with people she finds interesting. Noa is more affectionate. Emma is not (at least this is how she is with her family at home). But Emma is very attentive when it comes to her abuela. When they go out, she'll hold her hand and makes sure she is walking safely. She sees her abuela as "old" and that is why she likes to assist her (even though Abuela is only sixty-nine years old, healthy and strong).

These two sisters highlight the fact that although individuals with ASD share common traits, they are as unique and individual as any high school student. Both have their talents and strengths, and both have things they are currently working on making stronger. In both cases, their teachers give rave reviews about their performance in high school.[9]

autism. So a 7 percent relationship is much higher and suggests that this is not a random event. In addition, researchers found that when siblings shared a mother, but not a father, there was a 2.4 percent chance that the second child would have autism. Again that is twice the general population. This means that there may be something in utero also influencing the development of autism.

There seems to be a connection between ASD and siblings. If that is the case, why not look at their genes and find the ones that are damaged or changed in some way? Well, there are twenty-four thousand genes in your makeup. But still, scientists should be able to spot patterns using the latest scientific methods. That's just what they did. When looking at the genes of siblings it turns out about 70 percent

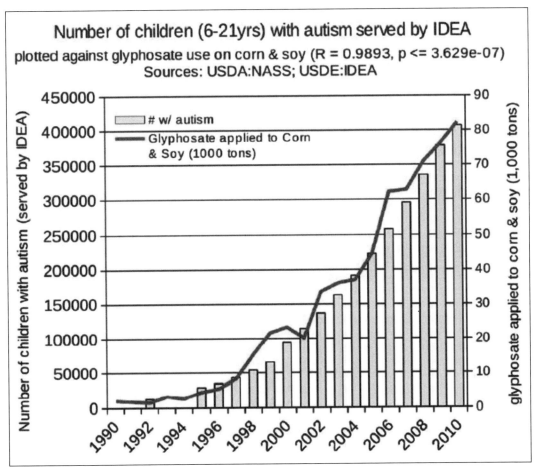

Glyphosate is a broad spectrum herbicide used to kill weeds. It was quickly adopted by farmers for commercial use. It appears on the commercial market under many names. The line on the graph shows the rise in glyphosate from 1990 to 2010. The bar graph shows autism cases in the United States. Notice anything? While we can say these increases are similar, we can't say one is causing the other. Lots of things other than glyphosate may follow this upward trend. Only through careful research will we find the cause. *Reproduced courtesy of Nancy Swanson, "Genetically Engineered Crops, Glyphosate and the Deterioration of Health in the United States of America,"* Journal of Organic Systems *9, no. 2 (2014): 6–37*

of the time, the siblings shared no similar gene mutations. Not even one. Thirty percent did share gene mutations. But from one family to the next there was no one or two genes that were similar that could be identified as "the gene" or "the pattern of genes." Meaning? While it is clear that genetic mutations are identified in people with autism, there is no single gene or single set of genes responsible. There are not even two or three. There are genes that show up frequently as mutations, referred to as known markers of autism. But in some people with autism, those genes are fine. So for autism some genes may be altered, but they vary from person to person.

What about biology? Maybe environmental factors like pollution or toxins, chemicals, pesticides, and other known factors bad for one's health could be responsible. Could autism be the result of a mother eating foods with pesticides that change the in utero development of the child? As you guessed, there are many studies to find out if there is an influence. As of 2015, environmental factors have only slightly been connected to autism. We also have to remember that there are thousands of environmental toxins. So far, only a fraction have been studied.

The environmental factors that research most strongly links to autism are influences such as birth complications (such as oxygen deprivation or maternal infection). Parental age is also a factor for both mothers and fathers. Parents who wait less than a year to have another child also seem to be at risk. This may be due to the mother's body not having enough time to recoup healthy levels of nutrients. Interestingly, there is strong evidence that women who take prenatal vitamins before a child's birth reduce the odds that their child will have autism.

The facts will keep coming as research continues. It is clear at this point we have learned a lot but still have a long way to go in terms of understanding ASD completely.

THE BRAIN AND ASD

Up until about 2014 most scientists thought that the brains of people with autism spectrum disorder (ASD) were larger than those without ASD. Why? There were studies comparing the brains of these two groups. They consistently found a significant difference in size. In one case, they found that differences in brain sizes did not show up until about the age of two years. These studies generally compared thirty or forty people at a time. They examined the size, shape, volume, and features using a technique called magnetic resonance imaging (MRI).

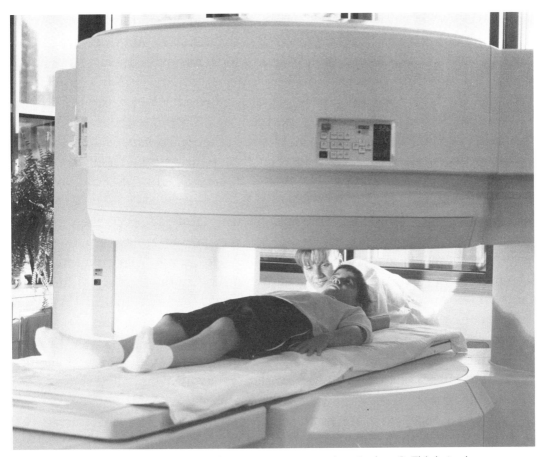

Magnetic resonance imaging (MRI) is a common procedure today. © *Thinkstock*

MRI

If you have ever had an injury, you may have seen this machine in the hospital if doctors wanted to see what was happening inside your body. MRI is a medical imaging technique used in radiology to investigate the anatomy and physiology of the body. MRI scanners use magnetic fields and radio waves to form images of the body. The technique is widely used in hospitals for medical diagnosis, staging of disease, and follow-up without exposure to ionizing radiation. It is a way to take pictures of your insides without cutting you open.

Looking at the differences in brains was done over and over by many scientists. However, not all results were the same. In some cases, there were no differences in brains between the two groups. But other studies said there were. Who was right and who was wrong went back and forth for some time.

In 2014, Dr. Ilan Dinstein, a neuroscientist from Israel's Ben-Gurion University of the Negev, led a study of over one thousand MRI scans. Dr. Dinstein and his team looked at the MRIs of people with ASD and without. They broke the brain into 180 different regions and looked at the size, shape, volume, surface area, and thickness. What they found was that there were no significant differences between the two groups. The brains of persons with ASD did not differ from those without ASD.[1]

No difference. Well, that isn't entirely true. You see, everyone's brain is different—no two brains are alike—and so every person has a uniquely shaped brain. But those differences are from person to person, not from group to group. Those previous studies probably just captured the natural diversity of anatomical brain structures. Most brains are very different from one another. My brain and yours may be 10 to 20 percent similar, but that means our brains are 80 to 90 percent different.

Dr. Dinstein's study came out in October of 2014. Two months later another study came out that may give a bit more clarity on why many initial studies were finding differences.

Nicholas Lange, associate professor of psychiatry at Harvard University's McLean Hospital, studied the brain MRIs of one hundred males with ASD aged three to thirty-five years and compared them to MRIs of typically developing males.[2]

The unique piece of his study was that it compared brain MRIs over time. He found that before age ten, the total brain volume tends to be larger in the group of males with ASD compared to males without ASD. The brains of boys with ASD actually grow faster. But between the ages of ten and fifteen, those brains without ASD catch up. The brains of those without ASD continue growing into the males' twenties. This is not true for the boys with ASD. In fact, their brains begin to shrink.

OK, so now you are saying, you just told us that there are no differences. What is the real story? The best I can say is that sometimes there are no differences, but sometimes there are; does that make it clear? Everyone's brain (yours and mine included) grows and then shrinks with age. But it seems (based on this study) that the brains of boys with ASD start growing faster, and then start shrinking sooner, than those belonging to boys without ASD.

So, there may be no difference in brains between the two groups, but it seems that there is a different rate of growth and shrinkage. What might the outcome be of this phenomenon? Think about yourself at the age of ten, maybe in fourth or fifth grade. The world opens up. You go from learning to spell to looking at more abstract comprehension of literacy, like the theme of a book or perspective of a

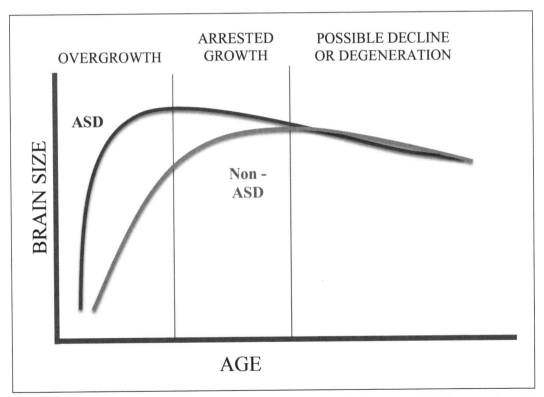

Everyone has a brain that grows and shrinks over time. But is seems that for people with ASD, the growth spurt in the earlier years of life is larger than it is for those without ASD. The beginning of the shrinkage phase starts earlier for those with ASD. As technology advances, so does our ability to look into the brain to understand how it works. *Courtesy of the author*

How Many Neurons Are There?

Popular scientific thinking had determined that there were 100 billion neurons in the brain. Dr. Suzana Herculano-Houzel is a neuroscientist who asked the question, "How do we know there are 100 billion cells in the human brain?" When no one could give her a specific answer, she answered the question for herself. She dissolved a human brain into what she terms a "brain soup." She then took a sample of the soup, counted the number of cell nuclei belonging to neurons (as opposed to other cells in the brain), and then scaled up to get the overall number. So far no brain she has examined has 100 billion, only 86 billion. Fourteen billion off may not sound like much, but that is the number of neurons you'd find in a baboon's brain.[a]

character. Your brain is growing at this point, absorbing new information. It is also handling more complex concepts. Without that growth, this new information and entrance into a more abstract world might be difficult to absorb.

Obviously, there is much more to the brain than its shape and size. The brain is made up of a jellylike mass of fat and protein weighing about three pounds (1.4 kilograms). It is, nevertheless, one of the body's biggest organs, responsible for our thoughts and coordinated physical actions and for regulating our automatic body processes, such as digestion and breathing.

The brain's nerve cells are known as *neurons*. They make up the organ's "gray matter." The neurons transmit and gather electrochemical signals that are communicated via a network of millions of nerve fibers called *dendrites* and *axons*. These are the brain's "white matter." More information about the white and gray matter differences will be coming.

Between the neurons are synapses. These are basically spaces where either a chemical or an electrical signal passes. This signal is what makes us tick. Your daily functioning is all about signals moving through the brain to various parts of the body. You want to move an arm; the signal from the brain travels to nerves in the arm and voila! Your arm moves. (There is a bit more to it, but you get the picture.)

Synaptic connections between neurons are believed to be altered in ASD. There can be too many or too few synapses, or synapses may be too strong or too weak or even occur at the wrong place. What's more, the balance between excitatory and inhibitory synapses may be abnormal (excitatory helps increase the

What Can We See?

Imagine that you compared two brain scans—one from a person with ASD and one without ASD. You could ask them questions or have them imagine situations while watching which areas of the brain light up during the scan. Electrical impulses are monitored as subjects go through these tests. There are consistent differences between groups (ASD and non-ASD) in the "lighting up" of the brain. Some studies have shown that the impulses are not as strong in people with ASD compared to those without. In other cases, one area of the brain may light up for those with ASD while a different area lights up for those without, even though the task is the same!

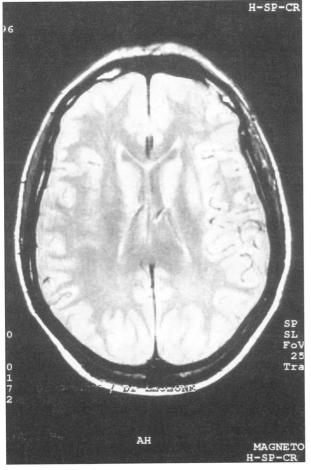

Scientists can not only look into the brain, but they can track the areas that are active during various tasks. This helps researchers to understand what different parts of the brain are responsible for. © *Thinkstock*

chemical or electrical action; inhibitory decreases it). That balance is thought to be important for establishing critical periods, the developmental windows where our environment has the most influence on our brain circuits.

To test this hypothesis, scientists use functional magnetic resonance imaging (fMRI), which follows the same principle as MRI but fMRI can look at the blood flow in the brain. Neuron activity increases blood flow. So if we look at the blood flow and compare groups with and without ASD, there would be a difference. Study after study say there is a difference.

Scientists have basically broken the brain into major parts, which can help us examine what does what as far as the brain is concerned. There is the frontal lobe, seat of reason and organization; the temporal lobe, seat of hearing; the parietal lobe, home to balance; and the occipital lobe, vision center. In addition to the four lobes, there is the corpus callosum, the network of cables connecting the left and right side of the brain, and the cerebellum, home to basic life functions like breathing. Each of the four lobes has a left and right hemisphere. Now, these are seriously broad strokes to describe the complexity of the brain, but let's look at

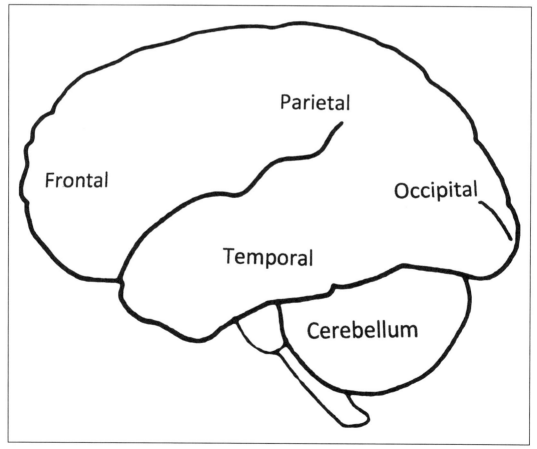

While each lobe of the brain has general responsibilities, all the lobes work together to carry out basic functions. *Courtesy of the author*

these parts and see what differences exist between people with ASD and people without ASD.

The Frontal Lobe

The frontal lobe is the part of the brain that controls important skills for humans, such as emotions, problem solving, memory, and language. It also regulates our judgment and social behavior. It is the seat of our personality and our ability to communicate. Since we know there are social impairments in ASD, it would stand to reason that this area would be different for those with ASD.

The frontal lobe also acts as your censor. You may see a video game or a nice pair of sneakers in a store, but you don't just take them and walk out of the store. You want them, but your frontal lobe reminds you of the rules and norms of society. We know that damage to the frontal lobe causes impulse control issues, noncompliance with rules, dramatic changes in social behavior, attention disorders, and careless risk taking. Similarly to the outcomes of ASD, frontal lobe damage may result in limited facial expression, difficulty with speech, impact on flexible thinking, and difficulty with environmental feedback.

Some research points to the fact that there are far too many tight connections in frontal-lobe circuits and too few long-distance links between the frontal lobe and the rest of the brain. This may cause some of the language and social problems and repetitive behavior seen in ASDs, according to a study published in *Science Translational Medicine*. This underconnectivity may affect the brain's ability to communicate information between the frontal lobe of the brain and other areas. It therefore affects behavioral performance in any of the thinking tasks when the frontal lobe is needed. In fact, most of the symptoms of ASD can be explained by deficits in the frontal lobe (as well as the temporal lobe).[3]

The Temporal Lobe

The temporal lobe sits closest to the ears, so guess what? Yes, it does play a part in moving sound. Most important is that it combines visual and auditory information. It also aids in the recognition of complex visual input like the recognition of faces. The temporal lobe makes it possible for us to understand sound, including speech. Our comprehension of language sits here. Things like pitch, tone, and volume are also registered here.

Many studies have found a decreased blood flow (thus, low neuron activity) within the temporal lobe in people with ASD. Indeed, autistic behavior has been associated with several clinical conditions resulting in temporal lobe damage, such as epilepsy and encephalitis. Furthermore, neuroimaging studies have shown an association between temporal lobe abnormalities and the occurrence of infantile spasms. In addition, experiments with primates have shown that temporal lesions cause behavioral disturbances very similar to those seen in autistic children.[4]

What are those behaviors affected by temporal lobe deficits? When this lobe is disrupted, auditory sensation and perception are altered. It becomes tough for the individual to maintain attention selectively, so when speaking to a person with ASD, he may have trouble filtering out all the other sounds in the environment. It is the same thing for visual perception. A person with ASD may have trouble looking at a board in class due to decreased temporal lobe effectiveness. Temporal lobe deficits also lead to organization and categorization difficulties. So being able to organize information becomes difficult. When you hear the word *dog*, your brain automatically goes into a filing system. It opens the drawer labeled Mammals or Animals, then goes into the subfolder of Domestic Animals, then finds the Dog folder, and opens a photo for you to comprehend. Not so when temporal lobes are affected. Imagine looking for the meaning of the word *dog* in thousands of pages of information, without a filing system. Finally, temporal lobe deficits lead to altered behaviors and mood resulting in heightened or reduced emotional regulation.

Parietal Lobe

Spatial recognition, sense of navigation, and the major receptive area for the sense of touch are all located in the parietal lobe. It integrates senses such as taste and temperature. Some language processing also happens here. But basically it is like the train station through which much of our sensory information passes and integrates.

People with ASD, it seems, have an interesting phenomenon with their parietal lobe. In the earlier discussion on brain nerve cells and fibers, gray and white matter were mentioned. Gray matter is basically the collection of cell bodies. White matter is the collection of axons (points where electrical and chemical messages are sent). The brains of persons with ASD seem to have more gray matter than those of people without ASD. In addition, the larger the gray matter, the more stereotyped behaviors associated with ASD were found in the individual. Other studies have found that the volume of the parietal lobe was less in individuals with ASD. This may be due to early development or early atrophy (shrinkage). Remember, those with ASD have an earlier onset of brain shrinkage than those without.

Occipital Lobe

Like the name suggests, the occipital lobe refers to the eyes, sight, and visual special perception. Strange that it sits in the back of the brain and not closer to the eyes, but there is a reason. You see, there is not one nerve running from the eyes to the occipital lobe. The nerves from the eyes (optic nerves) pass through all the other lobes, integrating and coordinating the sight to sound, to motion, to color, to just about every necessary area to interpret and understand what we see.

There are many regions in the occipital lobe, and these are specialized for different visual tasks such as visuospatial processing (seeing items and judging the space between them), color differentiation, and motion perception. Seeing isn't just pictures. Seeing an object move is controlled in one area, whereas seeing an object stationary is in another.

In an important study, researchers used fifteen years of data that covered the ways the brains of people with ASD work when interpreting faces, objects, and written words. The data came from twenty-six independent brain imaging studies that looked at a total of 357 people with ASD and 370 without. They observed more neural activity in the temporal and occipital regions and less activity in the frontal for those with ASD compared to those without ASD. The temporal and occipital regions are typically involved in perceiving and recognizing patterns and objects.[5]

The stronger engagement of the visual processing brain areas associated with ASD seems to match the theory that people with ASD have heightened visual processing abilities. This means the brain may have reorganized its pathways to favor the perception processes (or how things are recorded by the brain). A heightened storage of data exists in the brain. But the flow or ability to retrieve this information is still compromised.

Pruning

When a tree or a plant grows, gardeners implement something called pruning. It is where the gardener trims branches and parts of the plant. By cutting, the gardener is actually promoting healthy growth. Think about it. When you have a bush in your front yard and don't trim it, it grows into a wild shape, with parts sticking out everywhere. When you don't prune the bush, parts end up dying off because things like the amount of water and soil nutrients may not feed the whole plant. Once a part dies, it may affect the entire bush. Certainly, there is no control over the shape. Pruning to a specific shape and size creates a healthy plant.

Guess what else needs pruning? Your brain. Just like in gardening, your brain prunes itself. It removes the unnecessary connections and strengthens the necessary ones. Most of this happens between the ages of three and sixteen years. It happens in various parts of the brain at different times. Pruning allows the brain to maximize efficiency by creating strong pathways of neurons.

What is really interesting is that some of this pruning happens as a result of a child's experience. During early brain development, there are sensitive periods

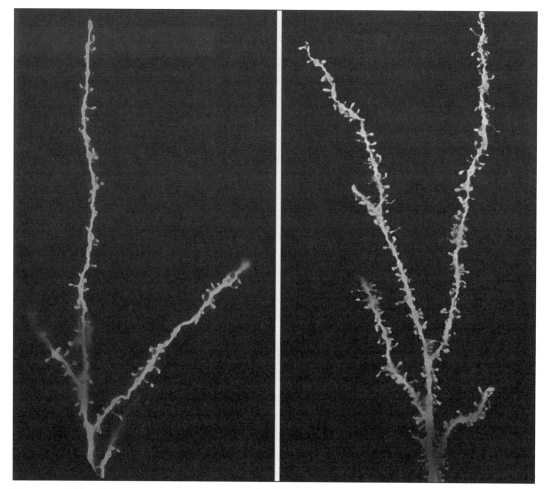

Can you tell which neuron was pruned and which one wasn't? The one on the left has less spikey parts on the branches (called dendrites), representing the pruning process from a typical brain. On the right is a neuron from the brain of a person with ASD. Notice the larger amount of spikes. Each spike is a synapse. With so many more pathways to send information, efficiency and strength are lost. By the time one is sixteen, those spikes should decrease by half. For people with ASD, they only drop 16 percent. *Pruning Photo Reprinted courtesy of Guomei Tang and Mark S. Sonders, Columbia University Medical Center*

where one's life experiences can affect this development. Certain experiences are essential for a brain to develop, like movement, communication, and so on. As the individual experiences these environmental experiences, the brain makes the connections to strengthen these areas and removes those neurons that are not being used.

For people with ASD, the brain pruning may be a problem. It has been shown that the brains of people with ASD have not been pruned properly; thus there are lots of pathways that are not efficient and not very strong. You have read about the weaknesses of electrical activity for people with ASD. Maybe this is the reason that the activity is weak in the first place.

Why does pruning happen? There is something called *autophagy*. It is a Greek term meaning "self-eating." Sounds like a bad horror film, but what it means is that the cells in the brain use autophagy to degrade or break down those extra spikes. The brains of people with ASD were found to be very deficient in autophagy pathways.

Pruning Other Rare Neurological Disorders

By studying other rare neurological disorders that produce symptoms similar to those in ASD, researchers have begun to find out some interesting things. Disorders such as Rett syndrome, fragile X syndrome, tuberous sclerosis complex, and Angelman syndrome produce behavior that is very similar to some of those associated with ASD. These disorders have been associated with one deficient gene (unlike ASD). With these disorders, we see symptoms such as social deficits, language deficits, and other behavior strikingly similar to ASD symptoms.

Rett syndrome is a disorder that primarily affects girls. The single gene affected makes a protein that influences synapse form and function. The lack of this protein creates fewer spikes in the dendrites where synapses grow. Those spikes often fall apart, are weak, or don't work at all. In this case we have bad connections.

In fragile X syndrome, the affected gene is the one that restricts the manufacturing of proteins at synapses. In this case the dendrites (the branches) grow wildly all over the place. The neuron's ability to prune doesn't work, so the person ends up with way too many neurons. Like the brain with ASD, those connections are weak and not efficient. Fragile X neurons often look similar to ASD neurons. In addition, those with ASD and those with fragile X often display similar behavior.

With tuberous sclerosis, pruning is less about the spikes and more about efficiency. The axons (the nerve fibers that carry the messages away from the neuron to the next neuron) are not organized or bundled correctly. It is kind of like getting several pairs of headphones tangled. You can plug one in, but you won't know which headphones it connects.

In the case of Angelman syndrome, the behaviors look very similar to those in ASD. In this case the affected gene reduces the "self-eating"; thus, once again there is a lack of accurate pruning. In addition, this affected gene interferes with the development of synapses, so messages are not transmitted well.

These syndromes can produce similar behavior and create similar issues with brain development. They all share the commonality of disrupting messages traveling from one part of the brain to the next to carry out a task or regulate behavior. They also share common behavioral results like social deficits, language problems, rigidity, and so on. It seems that without the essential pruning of neurons, things go awry. Too few neurons or too many neurons or inefficient neurons really seem to impact behavior associated with ASD and other syndromes.

Overconnectivity

You read about less efficient neuron pathways. What happens when there are too many? Even though most research as of 2015 is about underactivity, there are many instances where overactive neurons and pathways contribute to the symptoms of ASD. It stands to reason that there may be (because of all those spikes and bundles of axons) an excess of information going through the brain. Quite often seizures, and certainly epilepsy, are caused by overworking neurons. All of a sudden many neurons start firing. The result is clogged pathways making it impossible for the brain to carry out any functions.

So when there is a situation where there are overconnected pathways, what are the effects? Research from 2013 revealed that many areas in the brains of persons with ASD were overconnected. In addition, there was evidence that the overconnections were most visible in the temporo-occipital region of the brain, which controls visual processing. Connectivity is a measure of how tightly in synch two or more brain areas are. When two brain areas increase or decrease their activity at approximately the same time, the regions are considered to be strongly synchronized. So far you have read about what happens when the two areas are not in sync due to poor connections. The more overconnected, the more severe the behaviors associated with ASD for the individual. This and subsequent studies found similar overconnected regions (although researchers also found underconnected regions, especially in the frontal lobe).[6]

It might make sense to think that vision is special in ASDs. Some visual abilities tend to be better in those with ASD, and there's some agreement that many people with ASD use visual processing even when a task is not visual. Given the overconnections of the temporo-occipital region it makes some sense, but of course, nothing is definitive yet.

How about overconnections impact on one's social behavior? Some studies say that these overconnections produce more information (even when the brain is at rest), which may be why people with ASD seem withdrawn (or historically, in their inner world).[7]

"It's very difficult to interpret the electrical activity of the brain," comments Paul Wang, Autism Speaks senior vice president for medical research. "It's not surprising that the researchers found differences between the subjects with ASD and those who weren't affected. But when the authors speculate that the Asperger's brain produces more information at rest, this is just a guess. Are these individuals thinking about favorite topics? Are they noticing things that other people don't notice? Are they trying extra-hard to interpret the social intentions of the researcher? We just don't know."[8]

In another important study in 2015, researchers found overconnection between the motor cortex of the brain and the cerebellum. This connection is responsible for sensory information and sensorimotor (movement and sense of movement) connections. In addition, like other studies, researchers found underconnections in the frontal lobe. The conclusion was that the amount of overconnections took up more space, leaving less room for other important connections relating to higher functions of the brain. The addition of sensorimotor connections may be impacting the sensory input of people with ASD. It would stand to reason that the overconnections would make one more sensitive or aware of sensory and motor input.[9]

If one combines reports of underconnectivity in adults with ASD, these new studies raise the possibility that brain sync may change over the course of development. What begins as overconnectivity in children with ASD may eventually turn into underconnectivity in adults with the disorder, this according to Vinod Menon, professor of psychiatry and behavioral sciences at Stanford University in California. What would be needed is looking at the brain of an individual over years and years of development.[10]

The Savants

Dr. Benjamin Rush gave us our first report of savant skills in 1789. He reported on the amazing "lightning" math skills of a man named Thomas Fuller, who otherwise could not comprehend anything beyond basic counting. Dr. Rush asked Fuller how many seconds a man would have lived if he were seventy years, seventeen days, and twelve hours old. The man gave the correct answer of 2,210,500,800. His correct answer was given in ninety seconds and even corrected for the leap years included.[11]

Savant syndrome was first reported by Dr. J. Langdon Down, who also originated the term *Down syndrome*. In 1887, he wrote the phrase *idiot savant*, which described low intelligence, paired with the term *savoir*, the French word for knowing or wise, to describe someone who had a superior memory but difficulty in other cognitive areas. Today we do not use the term *idiot* for obvious reasons, but the term *savant* is now widely used.[12]

A savant is defined as a person with a mental disorder who has a superior talent in one area, higher than the general population. It should be noted that savant abilities are extremely rare and not all people with ASD have a superior developed skill. If you have ever seen the movie *Rain Man*, you know that the main character with ASD had superior math skills. He was able to do sophisticated calculations in his head. While it is true that some people do have these rare gifts, it by no means can describe ASD.

Savant skills within the ASD community range between 1 percent and 10 percent. These individuals have an ability in some area in which they are superior. No matter what the savant skill is, it is always linked to an enormous memory capacity.

There is more information today about the brain, and one can see how problems in its development will impact behavior. But what happens when more neurons are put together in certain areas? Temple Grandin, who is a writer, scientist, and person with ASD, has written extensively about her brain. After having her

Meet Michael. This high school student has the uncanny ability to remember everyone's birthday. Michael is so good that he came up to me and wished me a happy birthday (on my birthday), but I had no recollection of ever telling him. When I asked him how he remembered, he said that I had told him two years prior when he was in middle school! Michael is not sure how he remembers the many birthdays he has locked in his head. He says it is just memorization. He doesn't see any numbers or faces; it is just a thing he can do. Along with his great memory, Michael excels in social studies, which is his favorite school subject. He loves learning about world cultures and different people. He would love to travel around the world someday. Outside of school, Michael's favorite thing to do is see movies and listen to music. *Courtesy of the author*

own brain scan, she wrote about how the tracts from her frontal lobe to her occipital lobe are much thicker than the average human.[13] Since this is the major pathway of visual processing, it is no wonder she has a visual memory that is far better than average. This gift of a superior visual memory has served her well in life.

Most savant skills are expressed within a few categories. The first is music. Some people with ASD have what is called perfect pitch. This means they can determine what note is being played at any given time. Likewise, they can sing any note on key when asked. Some people with ASD have superior abilities playing the piano. Several adults have been featured on documentaries about ASD who can play virtually any piece of music by ear. They hear a piece of music and can immediately replicate it. Others have superior skills playing multiple instruments. Art is another area of superior savant abilities. This usually includes drawing, painting, or sculpting.

Another savant ability lies within calculations and mathematics. Some people with savant abilities can calculate the day of the week for any day in history. For example, if I say February 2, 1992, the individual will say "Sunday." Sure enough, February 2, 1992, fell on a Sunday. Mathematics, including quick calculating or the ability to compute prime numbers, is another strength even in the absence of other simple arithmetic abilities. Calculating six-digit prime numbers but not being able to give a price for a common object is another imbalance of skills that is quite curious. Related to this is that some savant abilities show superior mechanical and spacial skills. Some people can measure distances down to the inch without a measuring device. Some can build replicas of objects by using found material.

Most people with ASD do not have savant skills, but many show a special skill in memorizing music, sports trivia, maps, historical facts, and so on. I have worked with students who could imitate the sound of dozens of microwaves as they beeped when the food was ready. Some brands use five beeps; others, one long, continuous sound. These students knew exactly which machine made which sound. Those students with ASD I have worked with over the years have often had a special skill with memorizing lists and information. I have seen students remember every Academy Award–winning best picture, every New York City bus and subway route, the schedules for specific trains, state capitals, and presidential information (like birth and death dates, wife's name, place of birth, and knowing all the presidents in order of their years in office).

In my experience, some of these skills have been truly amazing but cannot be categorized as savant skills. For the most part these students had very good memories and were not savants in any way. It is interesting that the brain is able to hold so much information in order.

Theory of Mind

A popular subject in studies regarding ASD is a concept called *theory of mind*. It is pretty easy to explain. Imagine you are having a conversation with a friend. You hear the words she is saying and realize that these words are formed by her talking about her experience. The words are a representation of her thoughts (not yours). You in turn understand and listen. You realize that the story she is telling is about her. You imagine how she must have felt. You may have even visualized her in the scenario she mentions. The bottom line is that you understand that she has her own unique thought process separate from yours and you can have empathy, you can take perspective.

To highlight this even more—imagine you have two friends; one is afraid of spiders and one is not. Now imagine one of these friends says, "I saw a huge spider on my pillow last night." You would react differently depending on which friend made the statement. To the friend who was not afraid you may reply, "Well, that's gross." You'd be more nonchalant. But with the friend who was afraid you might say, "Oh my goodness, were you okay?" The instant recognition of someone else's perspective and knowing he or she is separate from you is what is called the theory of mind.

Many researchers have claimed that persons with ASD do not have theory of mind. Thus, they live in a world of physical things but not mental things. The premise is that people with ASD lack the ability to understand that others have independent thoughts and feelings. An important part in theory of mind development is gaining the ability to understand *false belief*: It means recognizing that others can have beliefs about the world that are different from one's own. It means one needs to understand that people's beliefs are based on their knowledge, that mental states can differ from reality, and that people's behavior can be predicted by their mental states. Many experiments have been conducted to prove the false belief hypothesis. The first was conducted by Heinz Wimmer and Josef Perner.[14]

In the most common experiment of the false belief task, children are told a story involving two characters that is acted out with dolls. The child is shown two dolls, Jane and Mary, who each have a basket and a box. Jane also has a marble, and she puts it in her basket, and then leaves the room. While she is out of the room, Mary steals the marble from Jane's basket and puts it in her box. Jane comes back, and the child is then asked where Jane will look for the marble.

The child passes the task if she answers that Mary will look in her basket, where she put the marble; the child fails the task if she answers that Jane will look in Mary's box. The child knows the marble is hidden, but Jane shouldn't know because she was out of the room and did not see it hidden in the box. To pass the task, the child must be able to realize that Jane couldn't have known that Mary took the marble and hid it in her box. In this way the student understands that another's mental representation of the situation is different from her own, and the child must be able to predict behavior based on that understanding.

Another example is when a boy leaves chocolate on a shelf and then leaves the room. His mother takes it and puts it in a drawer. To pass the task, the child must understand that upon returning, the boy holds the false belief that his chocolate is still on the shelf.

The results of research using false belief tasks have been fairly consistent: most developing children are unable to pass the tasks until around age four. Interestingly in one study, 80 percent of children diagnosed with ASD were unable to do so after the age of four.

How might this play into the behavior we see commonly in those with ASD? Does not having a theory of mind result in the behavior we see in children with ASD? There are probably ways of connecting a lack of theory of mind to the behavior we observe in people with ASD. For example, behavior of individuals with ASD is often difficult to explain. In my work I have seen behavior that seems to have no apparent trigger. Many children with ASD will pace continuously back and forth. Others may have repetitive movements with their arms, torsos, or feet. There are also many inappropriate behaviors including the touching of genitalia, grabbing others, and hitting. The cause of these behaviors is impossible to determine. However, it may be that without an understanding that other individuals have thoughts and feelings, people with ASD may operate in a mental vacuum, believing that only their thoughts and behavior exist and not understanding that their behavior is connected to others.

Without theory of mind, individuals with ASD would have difficulty understanding the emotions of others. Grabbing something away from another person suggests that the individual with ASD does not understand that the other person will feel bad or violated by his or her action of grabbing. The individual with ASD has no perspective that will put him or her in another person's shoes. An individual with ASD cannot interpret another's emotional response. In addition, those with ASD cannot predict the behavior or emotional states of others. When working with young children I have seen the following scenario many times: A child with ASD grabs another child's toy. The violated child screams, grabs the toy back, and even hits the child with ASD. And yet, the child with ASD will grab the toy again. Even though the child's grabbing action will likely cause the same response from the playmate, the child with ASD does not make this connection because he or she is unable to predict another person's response. To the child with ASD, his or her behavior is separate from the response of others.

People with ASD often have difficulty with perspective taking. I remember observing students who, during story time, could not sit and listen to the story. Instead, they would repeatedly call out and yell at the teacher. In one case a high school student with ASD was listening to his teacher read a story. As the teacher talked about the character, he yelled, "I don't know who you are talking about. I don't know these people. This makes no sense." This went on during every read aloud. Robert, in this case, could not understand that he was hearing a story and that the characters were fictional. In fact, every time he read fiction aloud, he would say at the end of the sentence, "That makes no sense." He could not imagine or place himself in the shoes of the characters. In this case, the young man could interact well with people. He seemed to have the ability to understand the needs and feelings of others. However, once he was forced to imagine the thoughts of a fictional character, he couldn't. Students with ASD who need more support than this young man have more difficulty in perspective taking with other individuals.

If one cannot take the perspective of another, one cannot infer the behavior of others. Individuals with ASD have difficulty in this area. A person with ASD may see someone approaching, but not knowing what will happen next, the fight-or-flight response may take over. It may take repetition of an experience many times before the individual understands the intention. I worked with a young person named Emil. The first time I held out my hand he put it in his mouth. Through repetition, we began to shake hands when we met. Remember, my hand to him is an object; the emotional representation of a handshake was difficult for him to understand at first. Over several weeks he began to understand the greeting. In addition, theory of mind suggests that without perspective, an individual with ASD may not have an understanding that her or his behavior impacts another. If I hit someone, I realize it hurts the other person. Take away perspective and the concept that others have mental processes; the individual with ASD does not take into account that he or she may be hurting someone. It is not malice, nor is the individual being mean. People must begin to understand that many individuals do not consider the feelings of others because they can't, not because they do not want to.

Imagine how theory of mind plays out in a social situation. A person with ASD is in a classroom or at recess where many conversations are taking place. For individuals with ASD, it is just noise in a room. They lack the ability to understand the social convention of conversations; they may have a hard time with reciprocal language. Most social situations may be difficult for individuals with ASD.

Teaching Theory of Mind

Patricia Howlin, Simon Baron-Cohen, and Julie Hadwin developed an intervention guide entitled *Teaching Children with ASD to Mind-Read: A Practical Guide*.

The intervention was designed to help the theory-of-mind challenges for students with ASD. It provided steps on how to teach theory-of-mind skills to individuals with ASD while taking into consideration the developmental stages an individual goes through when developing the theory of mind. The program was developed for children ages four to thirteen. The instructional areas include the following:

Emotion. Activities designed to help children understand the emotions of others include instruction in recognizing facial expressions from photos and schematic drawings and identifying situation-, desire-, and belief-based emotions.

Informational States. The second part of the guide offers instruction in simple and complex visual perspective taking; understanding that "seeing leads to knowing"; predicting actions on the basis of a person's knowledge; and understanding false beliefs.

Pretend Play. The last section of the guide suggests activities to promote the development of play skills from the child's current level of functioning (e.g., sensorimotor play) to pretend play.[15]

The intervention includes steps on how to assess the baseline of the child's current level of functioning and how to track progress after each session. In addition, the authors suggest always starting a session with mastered skills before proceeding to more difficult tasks. When visiting most classrooms for children with ASD, one sees that these concepts have found their way into the educational system. Most classes have areas with costumes, kitchens, and other tools for conducting pretend play. Concepts of basic human emotions are generally part of the daily curriculum. In addition, the child with ASD needs plenty of time to practice these concepts.

If you are reading this book you probably take for granted how much you use your understanding of other people's thoughts and feelings to guide your social interactions and your continued navigation through daily life. To make things more complicated, these rules of interaction change with each situation. I would guarantee the language you use with friends is different than the language used with your parents. Try to imagine if you were not able to use others' thoughts, feelings, and emotions as reference points. How would you know how to behave? How would you know what was and wasn't appropriate in a social situation? A lot of work goes into helping children with ASD begin to develop a theory of mind. In the next few chapters some of the tools and techniques that may be beneficial for people with ASD will be discussed.

5

THE SENSORY STRUGGLE

Individuals with autism spectrum disorder (as well as other individuals with developmental disabilities) may have a sensory system that does not work properly. As has been mentioned in previous chapters, the system is often over- or underreactive to stimulation. These issues deserve their own chapter because the sensory system is key in understanding the behavior of individuals with ASD. While the sensory receptors are part of the peripheral nervous system (that is, everything except the brain and spinal cord), it may be that the central nervous system (the brain and spinal cord) are responsible for the problems with sensory stimulation.

Sensory integration, a term introduced in chapter 2, is a neurological process that refers to the way stimulation from the environment is interpreted by the brain. So *sensory integration dysfunction* is when the sensory input is not integrated or interpreted properly by the brain. The simplest way to describe and understand this is to look at the case of a neurological condition called synesthesia. This is a condition in which sensory input from one place ends up in another. For example, you hear a bell ring, but all of a sudden smell bacon. Somehow the auditory input (sound) got converted into an olfactory input (smell). Weird, huh? But not as uncommon as you may think. Over the years, studies have reported that the occurrence of synesthesia is one in two thousand. Others have reported that its occurrence is one in three hundred or even less. The most common form of synesthesia is color-graphemic synesthesia, where words or numbers are interpreted as color; people report that when they think of a letter or number they immediately see a color.

I can relate to this as when I was a child, I would immediately associate many sounds with visual images. Now, don't laugh at me, but when I was a kid, a yawn would almost immediately conjure the graphic image of a banana slice. The buzz of an insect would conjure a yellow strobe light. When I heard a bird chirp, I would see a river stone. Not any river stone, but the same one all the time. I had a picture associated with lots of environmental sounds. I was very aware of this as a youngster and assumed everyone had pictures that went along with certain sounds. I believed this so much that when another student in my class yawned,

I replied, "I know I have bananas, too." You can imagine the response. I am not sure I had synesthesia, but it was real to me. Sounds were pictures. Because this didn't continue throughout my life, I am not really sure what it was that caused the visual imagery. But I do know what it feels like to interpret sound as an image.

Synesthesia is a very direct form of sensory integration dysfunction. Imagine the neurons in your brain from the primary receptors (ears, eyes, skin, tongue, etc.) as a road. So you are driving down Sound Street; final destination is the brain, which will interpret the sound and explain it to you, or provide the right response (for example, a siren may get you to look up or get out of the way). While you are driving down Sound Street, you jump lanes onto Vision Street. Thus, all that information that was once sound changes to a visual stimulation. All the chemical and electrical energy goes from sound to sight in an instant and *bang*! You have a picture instead of a sound.

I keep referring to the word *spectrum* in this book, because synesthesia is one side of the spectrum of sensory dysfunction and represents a very direct issue. But there are probably a million different ways people with ASD can have their sensory system dysregulated (meaning mixed up). It is also difficult to know exactly what those uncomfortable or dysregulated inputs are. Many children with ASD seem upset or in pain, but the source of the discomfort simply is not obvious, nor can the children explain what is wrong. Thus, researchers look to those

Naoki Higashida

Naoki is a thirteen-year-old boy with ASD who communicates with a letter board. He painstakingly points to each letter as he spells words and phrases and paragraphs. When asked why many people with ASD cup their ears, he responded,

> There are certain noises you don't notice but that really get to us. The problem here is that you don't understand how these noises affect us. It's not quite that the noises grate on our nerves. It's more to do with the fear that if we keep listening, we'll lose all sense of where we are. At times like these, it feels as if the ground is shaking and the landscape around us starts coming to get us, and it's absolutely terrifying. So cupping our ears is a measure we take to protect ourselves and get back to grip.
>
> The noises that get to people with autism vary from person to person. I don't know how we'd cope if we couldn't cup our ears.[a]

few who can explain what their discomfort is and try to come to a better understanding of each individual's sensory issues.

What Might Sensory Integration Dysfunction Feel Like?

Certain studies have found that those with ASD are hyperaroused by certain stimuli.[1] Imagine your reaction to a siren wailing in the distance. You would probably take notice. If you were hyperaroused by this noise, it might seem like the siren

Carly's Voice

Carly is a teenager with ASD who types to communicate. She answers questions on her website CarlysVoice.com. She and her father are the authors of the bestselling book *Carly's Voice: Breaking though Autism*. Here are some examples from their book:

Q: DailyDose @CarlysVoice What do you mean when you say "i take over a thousand pictures of a persons face when i look at them"?

A: It's the way I describe how we see. All the images come at us at once. It is so overwhelming.[b]

Q: I have a question Carly. How do I get a teenage boy to stop stimming all class? He says the teachers are boring and its way funnier in his head! I'm sure it is but he's missing all his instructions and the lectures! I'm constantly redirecting him but he's missing so much! HELP

A: Ok I need to clear up a misperception about autism. If a child is stimming doesn't mean he or she is not listening in fact we listen better when we stim. I'm at a typical high school and I still stim in class. I just make it discreet like rolling a small corner of a piece of paper. Look you all stim too. Think of the drawings you make when you are on the phone or twirling of hair or pencils it's a stim. There is nothing wrong with it but sometimes it's better to make them discreet. What are the stims you do every day? Really think about it, I bet you find at least one.[c]

was wailing in your ear. In addition, you could not shut it off; it would remain in your ear, blaring. Your attentional capabilities (how much attention you could dedicate to a stimulus) would freeze, and you would be unable to refocus your attention to another noise or stimuli.

Attention is important here, because you and I have certain control over what we pay attention to, and we can shift our attention to various stimuli. Attention helps us to filter out things we do not need to pay attention to as we navigate daily life. For example, you do homework with earphones on, I would guess. If you are good at it, you can probably give the music only some of your attention and focus on the math work. In a restaurant, you can hone your attention to the person sitting across from you to listen to the person's words and not listen to the table next to you. If you can, imagine instead that all of the conversations in the restaurant are coming into your ears at the same volume and you pay attention to all of them at the same time (or at least try to). For those with ASD, experiences like this are not at all uncommon.

Go back to Carly's quote about taking a thousand pictures, and you'll see it is quite revealing. Imagine seeing an image over and over again, but each time you see it, it changes a bit. How would it be possible to process that much visual information? Some have reported that lack of eye contact is because people with ASD can't look at someone and listen at the same time. The need to look away and listen to the person's voice[2] may be so the person can concentrate without being distracted by the movement of the mouth.

Sophie's Words

Sophie is a young woman from the United Kingdom diagnosed with ASD. Using a communication device, she shares what sensory overload is like for her:

For example, in a room of people talking, my brain tunes into everyone else's conversation, and I struggle to filter the voices out. . . . When I get sensory overload it's like I have 100 buzzing bees in my head, and my head hurts a lot and feels like it will go *bang!* like a balloon. . . . I bang my head on things to try and relieve the pressure in my head, to try and stop the feeling. . . . I find it hard to talk or make any sentences. My speech just won't come out as I want it to. . . . If you imagine having 50 people trying to talk to you at one time and needing to answer every single one of them, then maybe—just maybe—that's a little insight into what it feels like.[d]

A good analogy of continuous visual processing is this photo of the tumbling man. If you look carefully you can see each image of the man is part of one continuous movement, but in this case each few milliseconds of his tumble is captured. Imagine being a person with ASD who interprets and overlays every millisecond of time to create a jumble of pictures. This photo is simple and beautiful. But imagine if this process never stopped. © *Thinkstock*

Another common report regarding how those with ASD process visual stimuli can be highlighted through this experiment. Follow my instructions and don't look ahead.

1. First draw three circles. Make one bigger than the other two. Make sure the two smaller circles live inside the larger one.
2. Next, within the large circle draw two ovals.
3. Add a half-moon in the big circle.
4. Now draw the letter "L."
5. Draw a straight line that bisects the big circle.
6. Finally draw a squiggly line under the big circle.

Did your picture look like this?

This face seems simple enough to draw. But if you don't have an idea of the big picture, the specific instructions don't carry any real meaning. *Courtesy of the author*

The point of this exercise is to understand how many with ASD may see someone or something; they may see it entirely through its details without being able to integrate it into a complete picture. Some people with ASD, such as Temple Grandin, have described what the world can look like for someone with autism who experiences visual-perceptual processing difficulties. In her book *The Autistic Brain*, Grandin writes about people she has met who seem to view the world through a broken mirror, or see Picasso paintings everywhere they look.[3] In her book, *Nobody Nowhere*, Donna Williams says, "Colors and things and people would fly, doors would get kicked in and sometimes faces would, too. But it was never whole people, only their pieces." Perhaps this is how people with ASD see the world, in small bits and pieces, unable in many cases to integrate these pieces into a whole.[4]

Other visual processing issues with individuals with ASD can include sensory overload caused by bright lights, fluorescent lights, and sunlight. Lighting can be

What Does a Physical Therapist Do?

A physical therapist (PT) is a health care professional who diagnoses and treats individuals who have medical problems or other health-related issues that limit their ability to move or complete daily living activities. The PT helps with impairments that are limiting mobility, function, and quality of life.

A PT is an essential person in the lives of many individuals with ASD. Part of the job is to help students with sensory integration. Many people with ASD have regular PT sessions to help coordinate and develop better sensory integration and provide assistance with compensatory strategies that can help people deal with sensory problems.

A PT will help a person of any age with enhancing the development of his or her nervous system's ability to process information in a more normal path, which may help reduce the problems associated with over- or understimulation of the senses. The PT can provide examinations and assessments. The PT is generally the person who provides the intervention as well.

When providing service, the PT can help the person with ASD improve participation in daily routines in home and school. The PT will work with a student through exercise and guided movement to help develop better motor control. For example, climbing stairs may be difficult for someone with ASD due to vestibular difficulties. The PT will develop a plan of guiding the student through the motor process for which stair climbing is necessary. He will then fade the guidance until the student can climb on her own. We may take climbing stairs for granted, but when you break down all the motor movements, balance, and awareness of space, it is indeed a complex set of actions that govern this movement. A PT is trained to break down and coordinate all these aspects of a task.

Think about the lack of social interaction those with ASD exhibit. A simple game of catch is difficult. A PT may help to improve reciprocal play with someone by playing catch. This requires a lot of prompting, redirection, and guidance from the PT. I once watched two PTs work with a young boy (about five years old) in teaching him to play a game of catch. One PT sat with the boy holding his hands and manipulating them to roll the ball to the other person. The other PT rolled the ball back. The first PT, again, used this hand-over-hand control to help the boy catch the ball. This practice occurred three times a week for several months before the child was able to roll and catch the ball on his own. This intense therapy was essential in getting the boy to have his first reciprocal play experience. In doing so, the PTs opened a world of interaction for the child that continues to this day.

The PT provides teens and young adults with similar treatment. Perhaps the PT will sit with a student to engage in a game of catch. A PT may work with an older student on how to learn to ride a bicycle. Using a three-wheeled bicycle for adults, this includes the PT tying straps to the legs of the individual. The PT pulls the strap attached to the teen's left leg and then the right to help the person pedal. While pulling the straps, the PT provides instructions such as "Look forward" in order to help the person integrate the many senses needed to ride a bicycle.

The benefits of physical therapy for individuals with ASD are well documented. PT can provide the physical exercise that benefits all individuals. For those with ASD, independent exercise is often difficult and needs to be facilitated by a PT. Exercise has been shown to help reduce some self-stimulatory behaviors of those with ASD. Other findings have shown that PT intervention helps with social behavior, communication skills, academic engagement, and sensory skills. When you think about it, it makes sense. Imagine having trouble sitting in a chair. You may be squirming, have trouble getting comfortable, need to move, or have trouble balancing. Do you think you could concentrate on schoolwork? With the help of a PT, people with ASD can learn methods for and gain practice in coordinating their bodies, and they can develop an awareness of finding the comfortable zone, all of which will greatly increase attention.

Overall the therapist's general goals are to provide the person with ASD sensory information that helps organize the central nervous system. In addition, the PT can assist the child in regulating or modifying sensory information and help the child in processing a more appropriate response to sensory stimuli.[e]

stressful, and this results in behavior to filter out the light, poor eye contact, and physical symptoms such as anxiety or headaches.

Environmental distortions where the individual sees the world in a distorted fashion may also occur. Objects are blurry, moving, changing; they can disappear. People may look frightening, stairs may look like a slide without steps, and walls and floors may swing and sway. Misperceptions can cause difficulties with sustained attention, eye contact, gross and small motor coordination, ability to interpret facial expressions, and poor social skills.

Print distortions make learning or reading difficult. The individual may have good or even advanced reading skills but have trouble with reading comprehension or experience strain and fatigue when reading or doing other activities. Building breaks into reading may help to solve some of these problems.[5]

What does your body feel like in space? Tough to answer. I can feel that I am sitting. I can feel the keys of the keyboard as I type. When I hit two keys by mistake, I immediately stop to correct myself. The term *proprioception*, described in chapter 2, refers to a body awareness. Let's imagine for a second that our proprioceptive system (muscles, joints, tendons) is off. Typically, if you write with a pencil, you know how much pressure to put on it as you write. But if your system is off, you may put too much pressure and break the tip. Or not enough pressure so that nothing shows up on paper. Another thing that might be difficult is walking down a hallway. If your proprioceptive system is off, you may not judge how far you should stand away from the sides. Many students with ASD lean on a wall as they walk in order to feel the wall rather than feel lost in the space. I often work with students with ASD who grab my hand. Not to shake, but to ensure they have a sense of where they are in relation to me. Without proper proprioception, you just can't tell where you are in relation to someone else. Did you ever step off a curb without realizing it was there? That initial "thump" hurts. You didn't apply the right pressure to the step as you walked down. If you could not judge slopes and differences in surface heights, you might have some trouble walking, or even be afraid to take that step.

If you had difficulty with proprioception, you would probably need to figure out a way to identify where your body was. You might deliberately bump into objects. Kind of like swimming with your eyes closed in the pool—you hold out your hand when you feel like you are getting close to the edge. You would bump on purpose to know that you have reached the end. You might stamp your feet as you walk so you could feel the floor. Clothing can be an issue. Many people with ASD like tight-fitting shoes and tight waistbands because they provide a compression to the body that is pleasing (although the opposite is true for some because they are sensitive to the touch of clothing on the body).

Chapter 2 also had information on the vestibular system (structures within the ear that detect movement and change in the position of the head). You may be terrified of rollercoasters, which produce extreme reactions to the vestibular system. But imagine being sensitive to this movement to the point where the slightest movement, or step, feels like a downhill ski slope. Now on a swing it would feel like the world was ending. You would probably have your head tilted because you could not tell whether your head was upright or not. Or maybe you would have the opposite experience. You may need tremendous effort to activate your vestibular system so you swing and swing, waiting to get the feeling in your head just right.

Gravitational insecurity is an odd statement. It basically means that the person does not have the confidence that gravity is going to work for him. Part of the vestibular system is responsible for keeping us anchored to the ground. Thus, you might live in fear that every time you jump, your body will keep going up and up and up, even though Isaac Newton says otherwise. Even fear of walking down stairs or off curbs, fear of being inverted, and fear of heights would plague your daily life.

When you add all this up, sensory dysfunction certainly impacts one's daily life. The smallest of tasks can be turned into the most difficult process for an individual with ASD. When we examine all the senses we use together, at the same time, the world can be an overwhelming place for a person with ASD. Of course, there are many variations of this. Remember the spectrum of sensitivity is very wide. What may affect one person might not affect another.

Sensory Gym

When individuals exercise the body, they go to a gym. When you need to exercise your senses, you go to a sensory gym. Many schools and private agencies now are equipped with exactly that, a sensory gym. This type of gym is a space in which the central focus is exercising the proprioceptive and vestibular systems. In addition, the gyms are equipped with visual and tactile (sometimes even auditory or olfactory) materials designed to enhance or sensitize a person to new input. For example, a sensory table may be filled with beans or marbles, as running one's hands through them can be soothing. One can find items that provide almost all tactile experiences. Toys that are hard, soft, squishy, rough, smooth, and so on are all put to use to help students regulate their sensory needs.

Within the room one would probably see swings, trampolines, climbing apparatuses, and plenty of mats and large pillows. In addition, there would probably be a quiet space for the student to relax or block out sensory input. The diversity of the equipment is important because every person who walks into the room is going to require different materials. Some will use it to calm the senses while others will use it to stimulate.

What Does an Occupational Therapist Do?

Many people with ASD will receive therapeutic services from an occupational therapist (OT). There are differences and similarities between an OT and a PT, and both people are essential in the life of someone with sensory issues. An OT will focus on helping people (of all ages) who have a disability or impairment that interferes with those tasks essential to daily living like eating, dressing, completing school activities, and working. The OT helps the student develop solutions to promote and reinforce life skills by working with the environment as well. Making changes to a student's environment can have a lasting impact on performance.

Where a PT works from a medical framework, an OT focuses on the behavioral aspects of a person. You may see an OT working with a student on handwriting. The OT will set up activities and programs to help students apply just the right pressure on pencils as they write. This might include providing a cushion under a student's hand as he writes to reduce the impact. Some students require special gloves or an apparatus to hold their hand in the correct position. You may see an OT working with a student on dressing. Putting on a sweater may be difficult for those with ASD. An OT will break the task into small steps, use a checklist, and reinforce each step of the process. First the individual puts one arm in the sleeve, then the other; then he puts his head through the neck opening followed by pulling the sides of the sweater down with two hands along his torso. Each step needs direct instruction and practice. At first the OT may have the child put one hand through and then guide the rest of the activity. In time steps are added in order to help the child develop the sequenced steps of the process.

An OT may go into a classroom and modify the environment. For example, the teen may have difficulty staying in her seat. The OT may recommend certain types of seat cushions that will be conducive to the sensory needs of the child. Slant boards might be added during writing time. A slant board is a simple type of stand (similar to a music stand) that sits on a table so the child does not have to bend over the desk when writing. It may make the process easier for the individual's writing.

Within the sensory gym there are special tools that target very specific needs of one's sensory system. For example, there may be a swing attached to the ceiling. For those with vestibular sensitivity, this may be a great place to practice small movements that can generally increase as gravitational insecurity decreases (with practice). For others who need more vestibular stimulation, the swing can serve as a way to satisfy the need. The swings can be interchanged with other types of devices. For example, a body sock can be attached to the swing. It looks like a stretchy laundry bag. The student climbs inside and can be covered head to toe. When suspended, it can provide a student with compression to help propioceptive awareness along with vestibular stimulation as it gently moves back and forth.

Within the sensory gym there may be a sensory pod. Essentially it is a "box" large enough to sit or lay down in comfortably with fabric or walls that block out light and sound. This provides a place for those who are overstimulated. Comfortable mats, music, and soft lights can be added and controlled by the user to suit a person's own comfort level.

Another tool one may see is a squeeze machine. The squeeze machine was invented by Dr. Temple Grandin (who will be discussed in chapter 7), a woman with ASD. As a child Dr. Grandin would seek out deep pressure stimulation but became overstimulated when hugged by someone. While on her aunt's ranch she noticed that when cows received their vaccine shots in a squeeze chute, they would calm down after pressure was administered. She decided to build her own squeeze machine that would duplicate this, and it was a complete success. The deep pressure from the squeeze is very helpful for many with ASD who are hypersensitive, and versions of her machine are now available for purchase.

Sensory Diet

When I first heard the term *sensory diet*, I thought it was an actual diet that students with ASD ate because of sensory issues. I was wrong. A sensory diet is a carefully designed personal activity plan created by OTs and PTs to be used by a student throughout the day to help keep his or her senses regulated.

A sensory diet will help those whose nervous systems need adjustment throughout the day find a balance. Those whose nervous systems are very sensitive may need a diet that helps them relax. They may have to take regular breaks in a sensory pod to block out input. Or they may need to go through the squeeze machine to find relief from tension or anxiety. A sensory diet has immediate relief. The activities mentioned in the Sensory Gym section provide immediate attention to the sensory specific issue. There are also cumulative benefits. Activities that put the nervous system in balance (blocking out too much input or adding input to find comfort) help to reboot the person's nervous system to tolerate

The Squeeze Machine

A squeeze machine, also called a squeeze box or hug box, is used in many programs for students with ASD. Several studies have shown that this device works in reducing tension and anxiety for individuals with ASD. Because the pressure can be adjusted and the individual is in control of the movement, the squeeze machine can be set to fit the individual's level of sensitivity.

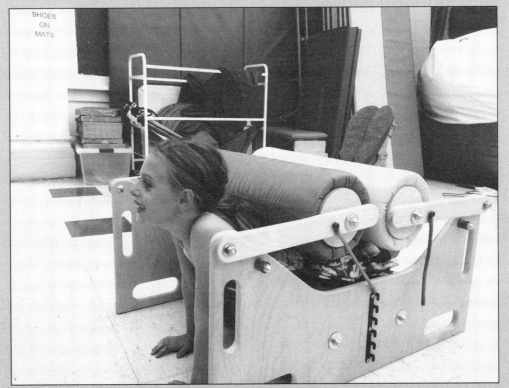

In this version of the squeeze machine, the user has the ability to control the pressure and the amount of time he or she spends inside. *Courtesy of the author*

sensations that may be challenging, regulate alertness, limit sensory seeking or avoiding behavior, and handle transitions with less stress.[6]

Creating the diet takes time and careful planning. Parents and clinicians need to look at the child over a period of time to watch for specific behavior and understand how the environment, the time of day, the tasks, and the mood of the person affect general functioning. It is not always easy to find patterns or directly

Sensory Checklist

These elements should be examined to see what reaction the person has for each sensory situation. The person observing would note if the child avoids or seeks the input or if he or she has a mixed or neutral response.

Touch

- Being touched on certain body parts
- Wearing certain clothing fabrics, seams, tags, waistbands, cuffs, and so on
- Wearing clothes, shoes, or accessories that are very tight or very loose
- Getting hands, face, or other body parts "messy" with paint, glue, sand, food, lotion, and so on
- Performing grooming activities such as face and hair washing, brushing, cutting, and nail trimming
- Taking a bath or shower
- Getting toweled dry
- Trying new foods
- Feeling particular food textures and temperatures inside the mouth—mushy, smooth, and so on
- Standing close to other people
- Walking barefoot

Proprioception (Body Sense)

- Activities such as jumping, banging, pushing, bouncing, climbing, hanging, and other active play
- High-risk play (jumps from extreme heights, climbs very high trees, rides bicycle over gravel)
- Fine motor tasks such as writing, drawing, closing buttons and snaps, attaching pop beads and snap-together building toys
- Activities requiring physical strength and force
- Crunchy foods (pretzels, dry cereal, etc.) or chewy foods (e.g., meat, caramels)
- Smooth, creamy foods (yogurt, cream cheese, pudding)
- Having eyes closed or covered

Vestibular (Movement Sense)

- Being moved passively by another person (rocked or twirled by an adult, pushed in a wagon)
- Riding equipment that moves through space (swing, teeter-totter, escalator, and elevator)
- Spinning activities (carousels, spinning toys, spinning around in circles)
- Activities that require changes in head position (such as bending over sink) or having head upside down (such as somersaults, hanging from feet)
- Challenges to balance such as skating, bicycle riding, skiing, and balance beams
- Climbing and descending stairs, slides, and ladders
- Being up high, such as at the top of a slide or mountain overlook
- Being on less stable ground surfaces such as deep pile carpet, grass, sand, and snow
- Riding in a car or other form of transportation

Auditory/Listening

- Hearing loud sounds—car horns, sirens, loud music, or TV
- Being in noisy settings such as a crowded restaurant, party, or busy store
- Watching TV or listening to music at very high or very low volume
- Speaking or being spoken to amid other sounds or voices
- Hearing background noise when concentrating on a task (music, dishwasher, fan, etc.)
- Playing games with rapid verbal instructions such as Simon Says or Hokey Pokey
- Engaging in back-and-forth, interactive conversations
- Hearing unfamiliar sounds, silly voices, foreign language
- Singing alone or with others

Vision

- Learning to read or reading for more than a few minutes
- Looking at shiny, spinning, or moving objects

- Participating in activities that require eye-hand coordination such as baseball, catch, stringing beads, writing, and tracing
- Performing tasks that require visual analysis, such as puzzles, mazes, and hidden pictures
- Participating in activities that require discriminating between colors, shapes, and sizes
- Being in visually "busy" places such as stores and crowded playgrounds
- Finding objects such as socks in a drawer or a particular book on a shelf
- Being in very bright light or sunshine, or being photographed with a flash
- Being in dim lighting, shade, or the dark
- Watching action-packed, colorful television, movies, or computer/ video games
- Having new visual experiences such as looking through a kaleidoscope or colored glass

Taste and Smell

- Smelling unfamiliar scents
- Smelling strong odors such as perfume, gasoline, cleaning products
- Smelling objects that aren't food such as flowers, plastic items, playdough, and garbage
- Eating new foods
- Eating familiar foods
- Eating strongly flavored foods (very spicy, salty, bitter, sour, or sweet)[f]

correlate a behavior with a sensory treatment, but in time through trying different techniques, the best results can be found. It is also important to look at the sensory input the person seeks and the input she or he may avoid.

Once the individual's needs are assessed, a menu is created that may include the times and activities the individual will participate in throughout the day. Or a sensory diet can be a list of activities from which the individual chooses when the need arises. The student may have a set of activities to choose from that would address a particular issue. For example, a student with vestibular needs may choose to jump rope for a few minutes when her or his work is complete. This helps regulate the body into the next activity.

Here is an example of a sensory diet that would address a student with a weak proprioceptive system. This particular student may need stimulation to reset his senses back onto manageable pathways. All three choices would have been carefully chosen by the OT and PT to make sure they met the needs of this particular student.

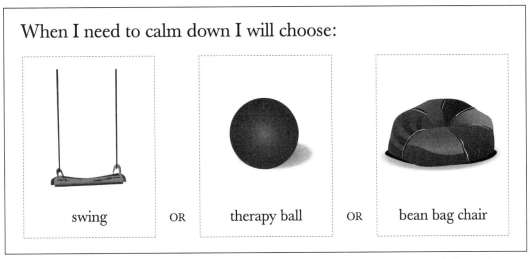

When I need to calm down I will choose:

| swing | OR | therapy ball | OR | bean bag chair |

Simple choices give the user a personalized sensory experience. *Courtesy of the author*

When I am finished, I will return calmly to class.

Date	Time In	Time Out	Staff Initials

It is important to track sensory breaks. It gives providers information about the frequency of breaks needed to maintain optimal regulation. *Courtesy of the author*

Sensory diets don't need to only happen in the school or clinical setting. They can be carried out in the home as well. Simple things like deep pressure application with pillows or pushing and pulling a shopping cart can target the system just as well as a swing or OT/PT equipment. There are mini trampolines that would be applicable for vestibular and proprioceptive stimulation. Quiet rooms or spaces in the home can be created that can help to provide a calming environment.

Throughout the day, parents and siblings can provide a person with ASD the regulation needed for a successful day. First thing in the morning, a brief massage on the back, hands, and feet, can help stimulate the senses after a night of sleep. Simple additions to routines, such as an electric toothbrush, are often a way for students with ASD to embrace tooth brushing as well as stimulate the senses.

After school, physical activities like swimming may be important. Exercises using the therapy ball or other items should be continued at home. Listening to music and doing art projects with clay, paint, and other tactile media can also be helpful. A warm bath with aromatherapy oils can be soothing for those with ASD. In all cases, the therapies do not stop at school. They are embedded in the teens' day and routine.

6

EDUCATION AND THERAPIES FOR INDIVIDUALS WITH ASD

Working with individuals with autism spectrum disorder can be challenging because, as you have read, every individual is different. ASD requires treatments that can be complex and require the attention of multiple clinicians. Time constraints, funding, and finding specially trained professionals can be difficult. Many individuals go through multiple service providers before finding someone who is a good match with the student.

From an educational perspective a classroom for students with ASD would probably look the same as any other classroom. In fact, approximately half of students with ASD spend at least 80 percent of the day in a typical classroom. Another 35 percent of students with ASD spend about half of the time in a typical classroom. The other half of the day is dedicated to the student's therapies and learning environments that are targeted for individual instruction. Only about 10 percent of students with ASD attend a special school for students with disabilities that provides specialized service all day.[1] In any case, those with ASD have modified programs to provide more direct instruction and more one-to-one time (one teacher, one student). Many students with ASD have an adult, called a paraprofessional, who follows them throughout the day to help with transitions, work, and complete other general routines of the day. Students with ASD may be pulled out of class for a period of time to receive direct instruction or therapeutic services by a specialist. For students with ASD, a typical classroom environment might work if modifications are made to help the student navigate the day.

For students who cannot find success in a general education classroom, some with ASD attend specialized programs that have smaller student-to-teacher ratios. Across the United States, these specialized programs may involve one-to-one teaching or classes with a small number of pupils. Within these classes, social

---

Noah

Noah is a seventeen-year-old young man with ASD. He is an excellent student with strong reading and math skills. Noah explains what kind of classroom and school environment are best for his learning:

> The maximum number of students in my classes [was] always twelve. It is a good maximum because more than twelve would make it hard to learn. Small classes are easier and people learn better. There is less noise and less distractions. The reasons why special needs classes should have small numbers of students is so that the students can all get help easier. A crowded class means the teacher can't talk with everyone.
>
> I also like nice teachers, teachers that don't yell. That would be a little frightening. I can't remember any teacher I had who yelled. A good teacher also has the agenda on the board ready when we come to class. An agenda makes it easier to know what is coming up. It is good to know what is going to happen. Without the agenda, the students would have a lot of questions about what was going to happen next. So, an agenda helps kids stay on point.[a]

---

skills, language skills, and functional academics are the priority. Within these specialized classrooms, activities and centers focus on the sensory needs of the student. There may be quiet areas, tables for individualized work, and other apparatuses (like special seating, bean bags, headphones to block noise) that provide support.

Lessons for students with ASD have unique elements regardless of the method one uses. Of course, the amount of support and structure will depend on the needs of the student. For higher need students, most of these lessons are going to be one to one. If not one to one, then small-group instruction will be used. Many lessons take the form of "say and do." This means the teacher gives an instruction, and the student performs the task. It is not lecture based nor is it full of language. Presenting one element at a time, with simple language, can be used to provide a clear unidimensional focus. Breaks need to be built into the sessions depending on the needs of the students. Some students can work for a few minutes, others longer, but in general the tolerance level may be shorter than it is a typical student. Lessons should include visual cues and prompts (which will be discussed). Many lessons start with the instructor actually holding the hand of the student to guide him through the process.

In addition, social skills lessons are as important as the academics an individual with ASD receives. If the student has difficulty attending to the task, like counting a group of items, the lesson may only focus on looking at the items, rather than asking questions about them. Once the student can successfully look at the items, then an academic task such as counting them can be added. For other

Pavlov and the Dogs

Applied Behavior Analysis has its roots in an experiment you probably have heard about. During the 1890s, Ivan Pavlov discovered that his dogs would salivate when he walked into the room. If you have a cat or dog, you will probably notice the same thing when it begs for food. Pavlov realized that the dogs had associated his entrance into the laboratory with feeding time, thus provoking a salivation response (a biological process necessary for digestion). He realized that this was a certain behavior that did not need to be taught. Along with salivation, he thought there must be other behaviors that are similar. These behaviors would happen as part of a natural, biological, or reflexive response. (Scientifically, the process of salivation, or any natural behavior, is called an un-conditioned response. This means one didn't need to teach the behavior.) Pavlov figured out that he could get the dogs to associate food with other things and start the salivation process. He began to ring a bell each time he fed the dogs. After a period of time, he then rang the bell without giving them food and the dogs began to salivate. He taught the dogs to salivate through the ringing of a bell. (Then salivation is called a conditioned response because salivation at this point had been taught.)

This experiment paved the way for behaviorists to begin to think about things like teaching and learning, motivation, and rewards and punishments. Thus, this was the first step to the development of Applied Behavior Analysis, which has become one of the most popular methods for teaching students with ASD. In addition, this method has been modified and shaped to be used for many other student populations.

students, listening to instructions may be the focus of the lesson. A teacher may have the student simply put different colored balls in a basket to get the student to develop her or his listening skills and to gain familiarity with the structure of sitting and paying attention to directions.

There are several therapeutic, educational programs for teaching those with ASD that are well established and well regarded that have undergone rigorous studies. Programs such as Floortime, Treatment and Education of Autistic and Communication Related Handicapped Children, Picture Exchange Communication System, and Applied Behavior Analysis are widely used by educators for a range of students. The most well known of these educational methods is Applied Behavior Analysis. Its long history and well-supported studies provide evidence of its benefits and have made it one of the most highly referenced programs for special needs students. We can take a look at how it is used and what makes it effective.

Applied Behavior Analysis (ABA)

ABA is the process where one uses reinforcement and other principles of learning theory to increase desired behavior or reduce undesirable behavior. By using carefully collected data, an educator can make decisions about an individual's progress and ensure that the presentation of rewards provides maximum motivation to achieve a certain behavior. Technically ABA can be used for teaching almost anything. It requires repetition, consistent application, and accurate tracking. There is enough research to show that ABA does make a difference when targeting a behavior to either reduce or increase its appearance.[2] Like the students themselves, ABA varies. It can go from a very rigid application to a very loose application. How it gets applied varies from educator to educator and from program to program. However, the underlying principles are the same.

Essentially these programs using ABA rely on the use of clear instructions, teaching small units of behavior, and repeated trials to maximize learning opportunities. Several research studies have demonstrated that ABA interventions are highly effective in improving IQ, adaptive skills (or skills associated with daily living), and social functioning when programming is delivered between twenty-five and forty hours per week. Research has also found that these benefits are generally larger the earlier the interventions are initiated in a person's life. Therefore, comprehensive ABA-based treatment is often sought out as soon as the diagnosis of autism is made.

ABA relies on a reward system, so an individual needs to be motivated to get the reward. Thus, the teacher needs to know what type of motivation a person has about a given behavior. There are two types: extrinsic and intrinsic. For the most part, ABA uses extrinsic rewards like food, stickers, positive words, or some other reward that the student seeks to gain. One may do chores around the house for money. In this case, the person is being extrinsically motivated by money to do the chores. But if one is learning to ride a skateboard and is working hard at it simply because he or she wants to do it, the motivation is not extrinsic; it is intrinsic. Something one wants to do because he or she has a drive or desire to do so will have its own reward. One would be happy and feel the reward of performing his or her first skateboard trick. ABA initially relies on the principle that a student needs an extrinsic reward upon completion of a task. It is often difficult to identify intrinsic motivators for students with ASD, so ABA relies on extrinsic motivators to produce desired behavior. Giving a student a snack or praising a student after he or she completes a task are examples of extrinsic motivators. ABA is a behavioral technique that was developed on the premise that students with ASD are not intrinsically motivated. Thinking has changed, and while popular thinking is that

Carly's Voice

The book *Carly's Voice* is the story of a teenager (named Carly) with ASD. She is only able to communicate through typing. And although it is a successful means of communication, the task of typing can be tiring for Carly. So, she does require motivation at times. Here, her father describes a scenario between Carly and her teachers, Barb and Howard, highlighting what motivation it takes to get Carly to type.

We had already learned that for Carly, food is a great motivator. Salty snacks are king. Popcorn, French fries, crackers, even pickles are her weakness. I think we could get her to walk across a fire pit of burning coals for a single chip.

"Carly, type five words and I'll give you the chips," promised Barb.

A small, sly smile seemed to cross Carly's face.

"*Five Words*," she typed.

Barb and Howard burst out laughing, shaking their heads in disbelief.

"Okay you win," said Barb, doling out five chips.

"*Just give me the bloody chips okay*," typed Carly.[b]

students with ASD are intrinsically motivated, it is difficult to identify what those motivating factors are. Thus by applying rewards, we can easily gain a response.

Thus, reinforcements that are highly desirable are needed to hopefully connect an action with the reward. In addition, there are other steps in the process of ABA, such as prompts and discrete trial training which will be discussed.

Pairing

ABA needs to be provided by someone who is trained in this area. Training is necessary because there is a very clear process on how to know when a reward will work. In addition, there need to be a set-up phase in which the educator uses the environment to get some insight into what may work for the student. The educator would first engage in the process of associating some meaningful, fun, exciting experiences with the student. For some students this is simple; it's a matter of finding out what they like to do through observation or direct questioning. For some it is not so easy, especially when they are nonverbal. However, even for those nonverbal students, a lot can be learned through observation. For a teen who likes to spin or holds onto a certain item (like a book bag or hat), the holding or spinning itself can be a meaningful reward. A very common reinforcer is to allow the student to have time to talk about anything he wants with the teacher (since some students have rigid interests, this can be most satisfying). Listening to music or using an iPad are other rewards that work very well. This is not to suggest that those with ASD are only extrinsically motivated. However, the use of extrinsic motivators gets students to participate in the educator's agenda. It is a way of breaking into a relationship. Once a relationship between the educator and student is established, it will be easier to move onto the next steps.

Prompts

ABA and ASD are extremely reliant on prompts to achieve desired results. Prompts are simply cues to learners that help them to answer questions in the correct way. A prompt can be something as simple as a direction for each step or a visual cue like a picture. For example, let's say a teacher is trying to reduce the amount of out-of-seat time a student spends during a lesson. The teacher initiates the lesson with the rules of the class (e.g., calm body, eyes on speaker, stay in seat), reviewing them verbally. On the student's desk are the rules with pictures of the correct behavior (thus, a picture of a calm body, eyes on a speaker, and a child in his seat). When the student gets up, the teacher recites the prompt "stay in seat" and points to the picture. The student may receive a reward at this point. In time, the verbal prompt is removed and the teacher may point to the picture. Hopefully in time, the

Practicing Conversational Skills with Prompts

Teacher: Hi Ashley, are you going on vacation for the summer?

Ashley: (No response)

Teacher: Are you excited for vacation? Say, Yes I am going to . . .

Ashley: Yes, I am going to Florida! (Reward)

Teacher: How will you get there?

Ashley: I will get there . . .

Teacher: Say, I will get there on a . . .

Ashley: I will get there on a plane! (Reward)

Teacher: That is great! (Shows Ashley a picture of a beach)

Ashley: I am going to the beach in Florida on a plane. (Reward)

In this example, the verbal prompts to the student serve as hints. Obviously, the teacher knew the student was going to the beach in Florida on a plane. Thus, she could provide the clues. She also modeled the answers by directly telling Ashley what to say. The visual prompt (picture of the beach) also helped Ashley to organize information and produce a sentence with all the appropriate information. All prompts should be faded over time. However, fading too quickly may result in the student making mistakes. Keeping a prompt for too long may create a dependency on the prompt itself. A trained educator evaluates how and when to apply prompts.

picture is removed and the student will comply with rules by using only a gestural prompt such as the teacher pointing to the seat. The hope is that after the student is rewarded many times for following the behaviors of the class, out-of-seat time is reduced (of course, careful tracking of this would need to occur).

Discrete Trial Teaching

ABA is based on its use of discrete trial teaching, which means providing a beginning, middle, and end to a task. By using the principle of pairing and prompting, the lesson can be developed. First, the student is given the activity or stimulus or task to be completed. This could be anything from a verbal question to a physical item, or even a worksheet. The student is asked the question and initially given a strong hint at what the right answer would be. When the student answers correctly, the reward is given. Incorrect answers are corrected and not rewarded. Over time as the answer becomes more reliable, the clues are withdrawn until the student can answer correctly.

Think about a discrete trial as an attempt or a "try." For every try there would be the reward for a correct answer or a correction for a wrong answer. A discrete trial may look something like this:

Teacher places two cards on a table, one with the word *stop* and the other with the word *go*.

> *Teacher:* Point to the word *stop*.
> *Student:* (Points to the word *stop*)
> *Teacher:* Good job!

A short pause before moving onto the next task.

Here the reward is a simple verbal response of "Good job!" For some students, this may be enough; for others the teacher might use food, stickers, and so on. But in any case, this is a discrete trial. The task here was to get the student to practice sight words. Perhaps the next task would include longer phrases or words the student doesn't know along with words already known. Regardless, the tasks would build upon one another as time went on and success rates were solid.

For every discrete trial there are five important parts. First is the antecedent. In the simple example, the teacher asked the student to point to the word *stop*. Without this antecedent, the child could not answer. This seems obvious, but remember an antecedent needs to be clear and direct. If a question is open ended or something the student cannot answer, he or she is not able to build. For example, asking "What do you do at a red light?" may not be an appropriate antecedent. That question is asking the child a comprehension question, but the teacher in this example was working on sight vocabulary. Thus, antecedents must be carefully connected to the task.

The second step is the prompt. When the teacher gave the directive "Point to the word *stop*" the first time, the student may have actually pointed to the word *stop* while saying it. Or she or he may have even taken the child's hand and put it on the card. The second and third times, the teacher may again point to the correct choice. After a while, the prompt may include the teacher pointing to two cards, one reading "stop" and the other "go." The student would then rely on the previous trials to find the correct word. The prompt is removed as the child becomes able to respond to the direction without assistance.

The third step is the response itself. It needs to be 100 percent correct. If not, the trial is not successful and needs to be repeated. In addition, the teacher needs to make sure she knows what response she is looking for. So, before getting started with the student, the teacher will write a specific lesson plan with clearly stated goals. For example, the teacher may have in her plan, "Student will recognize ten sight words independently relating to commands such as *stop, go, enter, exit.*" In this way it is easy to gauge the success of the student.

The fourth step is the consequence stage. There are consequences for a correct and incorrect answer. Correct answers are rewarded and incorrect answers are not. If an incorrect answer is given, the teacher corrects the mistake without reward. No reward is given without the child completing the task on his or her own.

Finally, the last step is the between-trial interval. All this means is a time between trials. The teacher needs to break up the tasks so that the student understands the stand-alone nature of each task. It provides a clear beginning and ending for each of the specific tasks.

It is relatively easy to remember these steps as the ABC method. A stands for the antecedent, B stands for the behavior the teacher is looking for, and C stands for the consequences. So in the example A equals the directive—"Point to the word *stop*." B equals the behavior—the child pointing to the word. And C equals the consequences—verbal praise.

Why does all this work well with students with ASD? Most people learn through play and interaction with other people. Students watch someone using a tool in a certain way or discover things with friends during science class, like problem solving through an experiment. Many students with ASD, however, experience social deficits; they don't have the consistency of learning from others, so teachers must force or encourage situations in which specific areas of knowledge can be covered. This does not mean that students with ASD cannot learn things on their own, quite the opposite; it only means the things that a teacher wants to teach need to be controlled in this manner.

The Story of Lovaas

Ole Ivar Lovaas was a Norwegian-American psychologist who is credited for coming up with one of the first programs directed at treating ASD. He primarily used ABA, and it was the first time this methodology was applied to a scientific research project, aimed at reducing inappropriate behavior found in ASD and increasing more socially appropriate behavior at the same time. His work was one of the first to claim that through scientific proof there was a way to improve the functioning of those with ASD.

Lovaas's initial research in 1987 compared a group of nineteen students with ASD, all under the age of five, with another group of nineteen children with ASD of similar ages. The first group received forty hours of one-to-one treatment per week, using the principals of ABA. The second group received ten hours of the same treatment. The treatment lasted a bit over two years within the child's home. (I will bet you can figure out what happened.) Those receiving forty hours a week showed the greatest gains. In fact, almost half of that group went on to obtain average IQ scores and were mainstreamed into classes where there was no intelligible difference between the students and their non-ASD peers.

A typical activity during Lovaas's study may have looked like this: The student and therapist are seated at a desk. The student (let's say a nonverbal student) is presented with two pictures. One is a cookie; the other is a pencil. The therapist says, "Can you point to the cookie?" If the child points to the cookie, then a cookie is given. (I am using a cookie in this case, but lots of things were used. Most importantly, the picture must represent a reward that is motivating to the child. If the child doesn't like cookies, there is no point.) Once it is clear the student can ask for a cookie given two pictures, she or he may be asked to choose from three pictures, or be asked to produce the word *cookie* in addition to pointing. This activity would lead into more complex pictures, which would help the student communicate. In time, pictures showing various items and activities would be presented (blocks, trains, stuffed animals) so that the child could use the pictures to choose what is wanted. Over many sessions, one would hope that many pictures were being used to help the child communicate basic needs and choices.

Lovaas's initial research had a one-to-one therapist working with the student in the home on a number of things. Most of these activities centered on daily living activities, playing with toys appropriately, and communication. A child was rewarded when compliance was met. Punishment was also used to reduce negative behavior like self-slapping and vocal outbursts. Lovaas's work included working with the child to break down tasks into single steps and build upon mastery of that task. So a student may practice one word at a time before putting it all together to form a sentence. The therapist meticulously tracks all the trials, errors, and successful completions of a task. Measurement is what gave Lovaas his scientific proof.

Lovaas's work still continues (although Lovaas died in 2010). The basic elements of motivation, rewards, and imitation are all implemented during the sessions. In addition, an emphasis on social interactions and cooperative play are an important part of treatment. To date Lovaas's work has been the most written about and duplicated study. In fact, ABA is the only treatment acknowledged by the U.S. Department of Education. In Lovaas's study, children spent forty hours a week for two years in the program. This is a great deal of time for a child to spend in such a program; however, if it is true that IQ scores sailed into the normal range, it would be well worth the investment. These methods are still employed regardless of age. For older students the tasks are generally related to age-appropriate behavior, like brushing teeth or getting dressed independently.

No research goes without being criticized. Lovaas's study was no different. First, forty hours a week is a great deal of time. The comparison group in his study got only ten hours per week of the one-to-one teaching. What if the first group had gotten eleven hours and achieved the same results? Are forty hours really necessary? Second, physical punishment was used in the original study (but is no longer approved in most settings; remember Little Albert?). There were also some issues with how behavioral improvements were measured and with how students were placed in ASD and non-ASD groups. Some in the ASD group did not fit all the criteria that would have qualified them (which were supposed to be random assignments). In addition, there was criticism that some of the participants did not meet the criteria that were supposed to be set for the study, with some students not falling into the ASD category.

Regardless, Lovaas's approach is still used today. Agencies and schools that use the technique generally build two- to three-hour sessions. Within those sessions students will work on a task for three to five minutes, which is followed by an equal amount of time in recreation and a longer break at the end of each hour. Like all ABA programs, tasks are broken down into small pieces and built upon after mastery of each step. All activities (including play) are facilitated by an adult, including a recreation period to help the student use materials in appropriate ways. (For example, an iPad may be a recreational activity where the teen can listen to music. The adult would simply facilitate.)

A Final Word on ABA

Try and think of ABA as a science in which the techniques are all geared toward the purpose of increasing desirable behavior. There are many types of tracking methods and types of planning that go into this comprehensive work. There are also many types of reward distribution and methods of withholding them. There are many books on the subject that an educator needs to be familiar with before engaging in the practice. Becoming a specialist in ABA requires specific course work and certification.

ABA is sometimes controversial. There are those who believe that ABA relies too heavily on extrinsic motivation. When you teach a dog to sit, you have a cookie in your hand ready to reward. This is often equated with ABA methods. Many critics say it leads to robotic skills that don't transfer well into the real world.

However, because those with ASD may have difficulties establishing relationships in which information is transferred back and forth, it is effective in getting the ball rolling. For students with higher needs, ABA can be exceptionally positive in increasing desired behavior. In addition, those with self-injurious behavior or behavior in which they harm others may need a fast and effective method to keep them safe. Students do make remarkable progress using ABA (and many other methods as well). Trained educators need to have a variety of tools in their tool kit when working with special needs students because as teachers have seen repeatedly, no two people are alike.

Picture Exchange Communication System (PECS)

PECS is a nonverbal communication system widely used with students with ASD. Developed in the 1980s, PECS is visible in almost any classroom; because most of the materials are free or easy to create, PECS is readily available for use in almost any situation. You have read about using photos or pictures during an

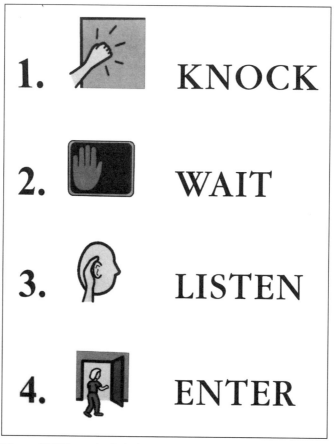

These PECS symbols help a student follow the procedure for entering the bathroom. *Courtesy of the author*

ABA lesson. Generally, these lessons involve a form of PECS to get the ball rolling. In addition, having a picture in many cases, even when a student can read, allows for a faster processing and redirection of the student's attention, making it easier for the student to comply.[3] PECS was developed as a communication tool for nonverbal children; however, PECS is now widely used as a prompt for verbal students as well.

PECS is primarily used to help a child develop reciprocal, or back-and-forth, communication skills. The student must first learn to give a picture of a desired item to another person, who will comply with the request. The person who receives the picture must immediately provide the item requested. Timing is important. If the student has to wait too long, the significance of the back-and-forth exchange is lost. In addition, the items that are requested must be available. The student will not get the lesson if the item is not available when a request is made.

There are six phases, or steps, in teaching students to use PECS.[4] All or some of the steps are used depending on the individual's needs. The first phase is referred to as the physical exchange. After doing some background work, a teacher takes the child's most preferred items and develops a series of pictures. The teacher presents one picture. The goal is for the child to pick up the picture and place it into the instructor's hand. Initially this process may be fully assisted by the instructor, who may guide the hand of the child to imitate the exchange. After repetition, the amount of guidance is reduced until the student can complete the exchange on his own.

Here's a sample exchange in phase 1: The child and teacher are at a table, and there is a picture of a snack on the table. The teacher helps the child pick up the picture and put it in the teacher's hand. The child then gets a snack and the picture is placed on the table. Most students will accumulate a book of pictures held in place with Velcro, so the student can remove each picture easily and give it to the teacher.

In the second phase the teacher helps a student to choose the picture wanted when given a choice of two pictures. The instructor prompts the student to pick the picture without assistance. The teacher uses two very different pictures, for example, a picture of a snack and a picture of a pencil. The child receives the item that matches the picture chosen. A child wanting the snack would have to pick the correct picture to get that snack; otherwise she or he ends up with a pencil.

In phase 3 the teacher adds the task of discriminating the item that the child wants from a much larger array of pictures. The teacher would start with only one or two pictures and then add others. Thus, the student must be able to choose the correct item from the group, which requires some focus and appropriate motor control. The teacher may also provide smaller pictures at this time, which increases the difficulty of discriminating one item from another. As the child develops the ability to request, the best-case scenario is when a student asks for

STRAWBERRY

PEAR

ORANGE

WATERMELON

PECS symbols help students make choices on their favorite rewards. *Courtesy of the author*

something not immediately visible. This helps a teacher realize that the student is now able to use more abstract thinking in requesting something that is not directly in front of him or her.

During the fourth phase a teacher introduces the concept of sentences. There are pictures that display the concepts of "I want" or "I need" that become available to the child. Using a sentence strip, the child must develop a full sentence in order to receive the item. First, the teacher models the sentence strip. He may first put the "I want" symbol on the board and have the student move the picture of the item to the end of the sentence strip. Over time the student would be directed to first add "I want" to the strip and then the item. During the fifth phase the teacher asks the student the question "What do you want?" and the student answers the question without pointing prompts or any delays. During this phase

I want   ice-cream

This sentence strip would be used in the later stages of PECS. The creation of spontaneous sentences in the final goal of the program. *Courtesy of the author*

a teacher would also promote independent use of the PECS to spontaneously ask for items.

Finally, in phase 6 the teacher expands this concept to other questions and concepts. For example, PECS is commonly used to teach students to answer the question "How do you feel?" The child can choose among different emotional

"Picture symbols definitely help remember things, but it is not really a 'high school' thing; it is for younger children, but some students in our high school use them. I prefer words only because words by themselves are a little more grown up.

Even though I have a good memory for a lot of things, I have to write down the instructions and the steps to help me remember them. In math when we do problem solving there are a lot of steps and I need to write them so I can remember what to do next."—Noah[c]

states all represented by pictures of expressive faces. In this stage the teacher also wants increased independent use of the pictures, initiated by the student.

Floortime

The name Floortime is most appropriate because just as the name says, this method of working with individuals with ASD means a teacher gets down on the floor and spends time with them. For young children it means getting on the floor and playing with a child. For older children it means participating in whatever interests the student. It is a model of treatment based on the premise that all students with ASD have interests, and it is important to help them develop their

The Goals of Floortime

The Floortime model helps children with ASD reach six important milestones. By following the lead of the child through interactive play and activities, the adult can develop the interests of the child and begin to bring her or him closer to these milestones:

1. Self-regulation and interest in the world. By adding new toys, materials, or manipulatives into the child's routine, the child's focus and attention can be directed by the adult.
2. Intimacy, or engagement in human relations. By joining a student rather than redirecting or forcing him away from his interest, the teacher shows the child that interesting experiences can be shared or even enhanced.
3. Two-way communication. A facilitator can add language to any play.
4. Complex communication. The teacher can introduce abstract ideas, for example, by using a block as a car or asking, "How high can you build?"
5. Creating ideas. In time the child can develop fantasy play or pretend play with the help of an adult.
6. Making reality-based and logical ideas. As play continues, the child will express play in words.[d]

full potential by first understanding who they are and then directing the students toward more complex behaviors.

When you were young you played follow the leader. You would follow the path of the leader and replicate his movements by watching carefully and anticipating what might be next. This is a simplified premise of Floortime. A parent or educator watches what the child does, and then enters into the lesson by engaging in the same behavior. For example, a child might be tapping blocks. The educator would also tap blocks. This would go on for a period of time, until the educator found an entrance to perhaps give the child more blocks for tapping. Here, the goal is entering into the play and building a reciprocal relationship. The child might tap the blocks and then give them back. In addition, the adult can add language to the play.

Pivotal Response Treatment

Somewhere between ABA and Floortime is a treatment called Pivotal Response Treatment (PRT). Like Floortime it is play based and child initiated. Like ABA there are targeted goals and behaviors to either reduce or increase. It was developed by Dr. Robert Koegel and Dr. Lynn Koegel at the University of California. In 2015 it was probably the most researched treatment for those with ASD.

PRT is used to increase and improve language, increase social engagement, increase communication, increase academic skills, and decrease maladaptive behavior like self-stimulation and disruptive behavior. The application of PRT is in a naturalistic (real-life) setting and in the home and is provided by an educator or family member. Children look at PRT as play rather than as the drills or tasks seen in ABA methods. The model proposes four *pivotal* areas (the P in PRT) that are addressed in order to be successful. They are responding to multiple cues and stimuli, improving child motivation, increasing self-management capacity, and increasing self-initiations. These four pivotal areas are believed to be the core components of increasing targeted areas for the student with ASD because they not only increase the skill level of defined areas, but also easily generalize to other settings and situations. In addition, once achieved, they can facilitate many behaviors. Unlike ABA, which focuses on a very specific skill (like sight word recognition), PRT looks at broad skills that a child can learn. For example, during a PRT session a child might work on increasing self-initiation, or starting an activity on one's own. This would in turn trigger a series of behaviors, like getting dressed unaided or asking for any item. Instead of teaching these individually (as in ABA), the larger pivotal area is believed to affect multiple behaviors. So, you don't need to teach the child to ask for juice, then teach him or her to ask for milk, then to ask for a cookie, and so on. Instead, you teach one skill—self-initiated requests.

First, the student learns to respond to multiple cues and stimuli. This first pivotal area is contrary to ABA because, remember, in ABA one would use a very specific script. Here, the idea is to provide the child with not one, but multiple cues. In ABA the teacher says, "Point to the truck." However, PRT would include asking the student to place the red truck in the yellow basket. Because children with ASD respond to a limited range of ideas and often pay attention to irrelevant cues in their environments, directions need to contain more than one cue or descriptor. This method would help students to listen to the necessary cues and ignore the unnecessary ones. Thus, the child practices attending to multiple stimuli that stand out in the directions or request.

Child motivation is the second pivotal area. ABA is pretty much based on extrinsic reward systems. For PRT the focus is on motivators chosen by the student. The child should be given a choice on the materials during the session. Objects chosen by the student will no doubt be of greater interest. Reinforcers (or rewards) should be natural and direct. For example, the reinforcer might be that the child gets to use the object she or he chose. Or the toys chosen are used to play a game with the teacher.

The next pivotal area is teaching self-management techniques. Like ABA, any behavior taught or targeted for reduction needs to be measured and tracked. But in the case of PRT internal rewards are paired with external ones. So a child may receive a sticker for being calm though a lesson. In addition, the student would be taught to identify the feelings of calm behavior. The child would routinely be taught to self-monitor so that the behavior can be repeated in multiple situations. The teacher must keep track of the behavior in order to see if they are being generalized into other areas and parts of the student's day.

Finally, the last pivotal area is increasing self-initiations. The educator must teach the student to make requests or initiate activities unassisted. Starting with prompts during child-preferred activities, the student would ask for the object before it was given, or ask the educator to join in play. Later, prompts are removed after the child has demonstrated this ability across settings.

PRT is tailored to the individual. One must be well versed in this method before using it. In each moment of play, the teacher is looking for ways to add requests or instructions that satisfy some of these pivotal areas. It is recommended that about twenty-five hours a week be dedicated to PRT. Family participation is essential so that treatment does not only occur in school; it happens at home as well.

TEACCH

TEACCH stands for Treatment and Education of Autistic and Communication Related Handicapped Children. While it is not a specific curriculum, it is a program of how to add structure to a student's lesson and how to organize her or his day. It was developed by Dr. Eric Schopler and Dr. Robert Reichler during the 1960s. The TEACCH methodology is a widely used program around the country. Even if programs don't use the method entirely, many aspects of TEACCH have found their way into classrooms, such as picture prompting and structured lessons. Developed specifically for students with ASD, TEACCH is based on those with ASD's strength in processing visual information, inherent ability to focus on details (rather than the whole), difficulty with combining ideas, communication problems, and need for or attachment to routines.

TEACCH developed a system called structured teaching, which is a group of teaching strategies based on the key factors of ASD. For example, all lessons use a system of external supports, arranging materials on a desk that are only used for the lesson or using seating that minimizes distractions. The physical boundaries of the workspace are clearly defined. All lessons have visual or written information that helps to reinforce the language used in the lesson. Things are labeled; visual cues with pictures are generally included in the lesson. There is also a structured support for social communication.

Students receive individual schedules clearly labeling the work activities. The work activities are laid out verbally and in writing (or pictures) that clearly defines what is expected of the student during the lesson, when it is supposed to be completed, and what would happen next. The goal is to foster the ability of individuals with ASD to work independently. By laying out every micro-step in a student's day, he or she will be more able to tackle these tasks independently. Each task and a daily schedule would all follow similar routines so the child's day is completely laid out in the same order and fashion day after day.

Overall the TEACCH system is said to have an impact because it was developed specifically for students with ASD. By looking at the strengths and weaknesses of the ASD community, the developers built the program by starting with the student and developing the principles based on the needs specific to ASD. Often referred to as a structure that fits "the culture of autism," this program is built around all the factors of ASD. Because many with ASD have strong visual processing skills, visual cues and photos are an essential element. Because of difficulty with reciprocal communication, every lesson features a language prompting element. Because students have rigid interests, the program allows for those interests in the lessons.

Here's a sample lesson involving one or two students with a teacher: On the child's schedule it would say exactly what subject is being taught, say, reading. The child would be presented with an activity sheet that would highlight the steps for the activity along with pictures. For example, the sheet might say, "First, student will take letters out of the blue bucket. Second, student will take cards out of the yellow bucket. Third, student will match the letters with the cards. Last, student will take a break." Along with carefully labeled containers and materials, the student may have additional prompts on the desk; for example, there may be a "help" sign to point to if he or she needs help.

ABA versus TEACCH

The TEACCH method is often less rigid than the ABA approach. In the TEACCH method, because the process begins with an understanding of ASD and modifies to fit the needs of the ASD population, the teacher is not looking for the student to meet a goal. Rather he is encouraging participation knowing exactly what will be needed for success.

Table 6.1 Comparison of Methods

ABA	TEACCH
Scientific Principles—Based on the behaviorist framework, the scientific evidence for increasing or decreasing behaviors is well documented. Thus, ABA used this theory to develop lessons.	Structured Teaching—Based on the commonalities of attributes associated with ASD, lessons are developed to address either building upon an ASD strength or modifying an ASD weakness. Methodology relies on what we know about ASD.
Skills Instruction—The content taught is very specific and well planned in advance. The skill is generally narrow in focus and built upon when the task is mastered.	Visual Organizers—By using visual organizers, the lessons can be implemented with no surprises or variation. The child, knowing what to expect, can participate and organize his or her thoughts and behavior to the lesson as appropriate.

Decrease Problem Behavior—With careful documentation, ABA can be effective in reducing problem behavior. Reinforcement and reward systems are tracked and monitored.	Prevent Problem Behavior—By setting up a system conducive to learning for a student with ASD, it is believed that problem behavior will not occur as the triggers for problematic behavior are removed.
Repeated Trials—Discrete trials happen over and over until the task is mastered.	Lifelong Focus—The methodology is applied to all areas of an individual's life and will continue as long as needed.

Medications and ASD

There is no medication for ASD; however, in many cases medication is used for specific behavior that is present in individuals with ASD. In fact, the Food and Drug Administration of the United States has only approved one drug for use specifically with individuals with ASD (Risperidone was approved for irritability in children and teens aged five through sixteen). However, other medications are frequently used for a specific issue. These medications are often prescribed to treat behavioral problems with aggression, attention, and anxiety as well as medical issues such as seizures. As of 2015 it was believed that about 56 percent of people with ASD take one or more drugs to control symptoms. Drugs by themselves are not the best treatment. It has been shown that medications along with behavioral treatments (ABA, social skills training, etc.) provide better results than just medication alone.[5]

Children and adults with ASD may not respond to medications in the same way as typically developing individuals. Parents who do seek medication should always seek out a doctor who has experience with ASD. The doctor will monitor the effects of the medications closely to adjust dosage or track progress. This is especially important to ensure the symptoms don't become worse.

Different types of medications handle different things. When you read the section about the brain, you read how complex it is and how carefully synced it is in carrying out our daily routines. Thus, medications (which affect the brain) need careful attention and planning. Many of the prescribed medications are not for use in people under eighteen years of age.

Serotonin reuptake inhibitors (SSRIs) are most commonly prescribed for people with ASD to treat the symptoms of anxiety and depression as well as obsessive-compulsive symptoms. They are marketed under many names, Prozac being the most well known. These drugs prevent the brain from absorbing serotonin (a naturally occurring chemical produced in the body). Changing the amount of this chemical in the brain may improve communication between nerve cells that regulate one's mood. These types of medications often can help decrease the repetitive ritualistic behavior in those with ASD as well as anxiety and/or depression.

For behavioral problems, antipsychotic medications are often prescribed. Like SSRIs, which reduce a chemical in the brain, antipsychotic drugs reduce the amount of dopamine and other chemicals in the brain. Antipsychotic drugs (like Risperdal) can help regulate mood, delusions, and thought disorders. For seizures, which are found in 25 percent of people with ASD, anticonvulsants may be used. These drugs suppress the excessive firing of neurons during a seizure. Those with ADHD (attention-deficit/hyperactivity disorder) may take a stimulant (such as Ritalin). It may decrease impulsivity and hyperactivity.

Along with these medications come side effects that may occur in the user. The most common is loss of appetite or weight gain. In addition, the individual may develop tremors or tics. It's possible that the symptom the medication is trying to treat actually worsens. In all cases, the doctor working with the individual must monitor changes to ensure that these side effects are not life threatening or problematic.

What's Next?

Right now, environmental influences, such as school programs, and parent work have had benefits in treating those with ASD. In addition, some drugs are also improving life for people with ASD. As the scientific community learns more about the brain, they can apply new ideas and research about ASD and hope to figure out a solution to how to best improve the lives of those with ASD.

Given what is known about the brain and the deficits in neural connections, why can't we invent a drug that would just make sure that the brain develops correctly in the womb? Is it possible? There is an interesting field of study that looks at prenatal and perinatal (newborn) therapies that may treat or even prevent ASD. In France, at the Mediterranean Institute of Neurobiology, a study was released on this topic.[6] It's a bit complicated, but here are the basics.

Neurons in the brain have a chemical called chloride. This can be found in high levels during the embryonic stage of development. GABA (gamma-aminobutyric acid) is the main messenger chemical of the brain, which excites neurons or turns them on during the time before and during birth. GABA does this to help build the brain. When GABA turns on, chloride levels drop. This drop in chloride happens at the same time the mother produces oxytocin, which drives uterine contractions. Scientists had known that high chloride levels had been found in those with childhood brain disorders. So maybe GABA wasn't doing its job. Maybe the high chloride levels were there because the switch didn't happen. GABA was not exciting the neurons.

Basically, the study showed (in rats, not people) that normal brain development could indeed happen by turning on a GABA switch in the brain. The scientists created rats with ASD by injecting them with valporic acid (a medicine used in the treatment of epilepsy, some bipolar disorders, and protection against migraines). Valporic acid exposure had been known to show a 4 percent heightened risk in ASD. They created rats with chemical and behavioral similarities to those with ASD. When scientists found a way of using oxytocin and a drug called bumetanide to turn on GABA and reduce chloride, they saw changes in the rats. Their brains went on a normal course of development.

Today there is no way to measure the amount of chloride in newborns, but trials of both oxytocin and bumetanide are ongoing for adults. In addition, there is no way to look for biological markers to determine if a fetus or newborn will have ASD. However, this new area suggests paths of research and changes in thinking that may inform the next steps.

THE FAME OF ASD

Many people attribute their success to having autism spectrum disorder. The unique perspective of these individuals, who share their stories of living with ASD, allow us to look into their world and see how ASD has affected their lives. The majority of those with ASD do not go on to celebrity status, but those who do set a shining example of the possibilities of growth and success for all people. Looking at the amazing drawings and paintings or listening to the music created by those with ASD is inspiring. You will read a few of these stories here. ASD is not always a limitation, but instead a gift.

There are many who speculate that Thomas Jefferson was a person with ASD. Obviously we can never know, but if ASD can somehow enhance a person's cognitive abilities to think outside the box, it is no wonder that names such as Albert Einstein, Wolfgang Amadeus Mozart, Isaac Newton, and Bill Gates have been associated with some form of ASD. Whether a diagnosis of ASD is true or not, these people seem to have a remarkable way of thinking that helped them to develop theories and inventions that enhance all our lives. You must have learned about Isaac Newton in school. Would he have been able to develop the world-changing theories about gravity without his well-documented social isolation? Social isolation does not mean he was a person with ASD, but that trait probably fueled his intensity toward inner thinking and compulsive work habits. ASD or not, all people have certainly benefitted from these remarkable individuals.

Temple Grandin

No one has given us better understanding about the world of ASD than Dr. Temple Grandin. Dr. Grandin is a professor of Animal Science at Colorado State University. In 2010, *Time* magazine named her as one of the top one hundred people who most affect our world. The same year a biopic of her life story was released highlighting her work as the most important scientist in the humane live-stock handling industry. She has written ten books and hundreds of articles about animal sciences and autism. She is one of the world's most influential advocates on the subject of ASD.

Dr. Temple Grandin is a pioneer the field of animal sciences. *Photo reprinted courtesy of Rosalie Winard*

You may not know her name, but you know her work. Dr. Grandin is responsible for designing half of the cattle processing plants in the United States and has designed plants worldwide. She has developed systems of livestock harvesting areas at meat processing plants that have improved the health and welfare of the animals we use as food. Her methods provided a safe and humane way of treating animals. The processing plants she has developed solved an important problem. Animals led through the processing plants were often experiencing high levels of anxiety and getting spooked by the process. The meat industry has reported that animals with high levels of anxiety have poor pH balances and high levels of adrenaline which produce lower quality meats.[1] Temple Grandin realized that this method of processing was inhumane and unnecessary. Thus, she developed a safe and reliable system that has saved the industry money, kept workers and animals safe, and revolutionized our food source. How she got there is a remarkable story.

Dr. Grandin was born in 1947 in Boston, Massachusetts. From the beginning of her life, Dr. Grandin displayed classic symptoms of ASD, such as lack of language, sensitivity to physical contact, explosive behavior, and a fixation on spinning objects. Her early life lacked most of the typical interactions parents usually have with their children. She did not make eye contact; she would fixate on sand dripping through her fingers and watch spinning coins for hours. She displayed adverse reactions to bright lights, loud sounds, and strong smells. Her responses were often interpreted as physical pain.

In her book *The Autistic Brain* Dr. Grandin writes that she was fortunate to be born in 1947, for had she been born ten years later her life would have been very different. Little was known about autism in the year of her birth; years later Bettelheim would coin the term *refrigerator mothers* (see chapter 3), which may have set Dr. Grandin's future onto a different path. But because so little was known, Temple's mother used her common sense and instinct and found a neurologist. Although her diagnosis was "brain damage," the doctor did refer the family to a speech therapist who worked with Temple and employed methods that are still in use today. Temple always had a difficult time hearing or processing the initial sounds of words. So finding a speech therapist was an important part of her early intervention. In addition, Temple's mother employed a nanny who would provide intense behavioral therapy. The nanny would spend hours teaching Temple table manners and how to take turns, and interact with her in a way that would promote appropriate behavioral techniques. In her book *The Autistic Brain* Temple writes, "I was not allowed to twirl my fork around over my head. The only time I could revert back to autism was for one hour after lunch. The rest of the day, I had to live in a nonrocking, nontwirling world."[2]

Had she been born ten years later and received the initial diagnosis of autism, she may have been sent to an institution because the problem would have been perceived as purely psychological. The brilliant mind of Temple Grandin may have been lost to us forever. Fortunately, her mother and those around her worked on the symptoms and helped Temple Grandin to unlock the amazing potential of her mind. The word *autism* was not used to describe Temple until she was thirteen.

Temple Grandin is a person who has an incredible visual processing ability. She can recall and visualize almost everything with exceptionally specific details. In his biography of Grandin, Sy Montgomery writes,

Temple saw almost everything in exceptionally rich detail. She could recall every image almost as if it were a photograph or a movie . . . her mind would run a videotape of images. Each image was specific—not a generic representation or an idea. Temple thought entirely in pictures. She still does to this day.

Most of us think mainly in words or ideas. When you hear the words "church steeple" you probably see in your mind a sort of general, tall white pointy structure on the roof of a house of worship. But when

Temple thinks "church steeple," she sees a series of specific pictures: the steeple on St. Paul's Episcopal Church in Dedham, Massachusetts, where she grew up; the one with a giant cross in Fort Collins, Colorado, where she now lives. . . . On and on the pictures go, like a computer search of images projected rapidly inside her head.[3]

Years later Temple Grandin would undergo a series of fMRI (functional magnetic resonance imaging) studies. Her exceptional visual memories might be explained by the fact that the cortical thickness of both right and left entorhinal cortices (the hub in a wide network for memory) was significantly greater than the average person. This larger than usual brain region is basically the funnel through which we commit things to memory.

School was, of course, a difficult place for Temple. She would suffer the teasing and name calling of classmates because of her odd behavior. Often she responded with a slap or a push, which would inevitably get her in trouble. On one instance when a classmate called her "retarded," she threw a textbook and hit the student in the eye. After this incident she was expelled. Fortunately, she was accepted to a boarding school which seemed to truly understand that Temple Grandin was a gifted individual and allowed her to explore her interests in science. The school recognized that although different, people like Temple were actually gifted in many ways, and allowed those gifts to shine. After graduating second in her class, she was accepted to Franklin Pierce College where she would begin her path toward a doctorate in animal sciences.

Inventor and Innovator

Since childhood, Temple Grandin not only saw the importance of hands-on learning; she also lived it. As a child she loved to build and create. She developed kites that would fly behind her tricycle, before she could ride a two-wheeled bike. She made parachutes from fabric and built a lean-to in the woods. Being so creative gave her a popular status among her friends. She would begin a project and have all the kids from the neighborhood clamoring to help. Her childhood bedroom was booby-trapped with strings and signs saying "Enter at your Own Risk" that would drop when activated. She and her sisters invented plays and created costumes and put them on for her family. In school she excelled in art and created masterful drawings of horses. She also loved carpentry class. She became adept at handling tools, building things that rivaled the great inventors of the century. In boarding school, she even worked with a group to design and build a three-hundred-foot ski tow.

Some of her creativity took the form of practical jokes. She would tie the window blinds to a student's desk so when the student opened it, the blinds would come crashing down! (Don't try this in school!) She would hide students' clothing during gym class so they would have to wear their gym clothing for the rest of the day. Her practical jokes, which remained anonymous (born out of boredom), were not met with great acceptance.

One invention that gained great interest was her famous "squeeze machine." You have read about the importance of sensory diets and how people with ASD respond well to certain sensory devices. Temple Grandin may have invented one of the first. The squeeze machine or hug machine is a V-shaped device that is padded. The controls at one end use air compression to squeeze the boards together, applying deep pressure to the person sitting inside.

As a child Temple often visited her aunt's ranch in Arizona (a place that would influence her for the rest of her life). She watched as cattle entered a chute for inoculation. After the shot, the chute squeezed together applying deep pressure to the cattle. She noticed that this immediately soothed and calmed the cattle down. She quickly realized that maybe this would work for her. Because of her hypersensitivity, perhaps a similar squeeze would reset her nervous system as it had done for the cattle.

Temple Grandin's Squeeze Machine

Temple Grandin wrote about her squeeze machine in a paper titled "Calming Effects of Deep Touch Pressure in Patients with Autistic Disorder, College Students, and Animals." Here is an excerpt:

The squeeze machine device developed by the author consists of two padded side boards which are hinged at the bottom to form a V-shape. The user steps into the machine and lies down on the inside in the V-shaped crevicelike space. The inside surfaces of the device are completely lined with thick foam rubber. Deep touch pressure stimulation is applied along both sides of the person's body, with lateral pressure pushing inward onto the body. The V-shaped space supports the body fully from head to toe, so that the users can completely relax. The contoured padding provides an even pressure across the entire lateral aspects of the body without generating specific pressure points. The foam-padded head rest and padded neck opening are covered with soft fake fur. When the neck opening closes around the neck, it enhances the feeling of being surrounded and contained by the embrace of the deep touch pressure squeeze.

The user has complete control over the amount of pressure applied. A lever-operated pneumatic valve, which is connected to an air cylinder that pulls the side boards together, allows the user to self-regulate the amount of pressure applied. For adults, the air pressure on the 5 cm diameter air cylinder is set at 60 psi, which allows up to 43 kg (95 lbs.) of pressure to be exerted on each rope attached to the sides. For children under age 8–9 years, the pressure is set at 30 to 40 psi.

The user can enter and leave the machine at will, which confers a more complete sense of self-control in the context of the machine. The squeeze machine and procedures for its use are more fully described elsewhere.

The advantage of the squeeze machine over other forms of deep pressure stimulation, such as rolling in mats, is that the machine can apply greater amounts of pressure over larger areas of the body. The air cylinder power applies constant pressure, even when the user shifts position.[a]

Temple Grandin first asked her aunt to close her into the cattle chute. A strange request. What would you have done? Fortunately, Temple's aunt agreed and put her into the cattle machine. At first her anxiety rose and she became nervous, but then something happened. Temple began to feel calm. She remained in the chute for half an hour enjoying the peace and security of the machine. During her stays at the ranch, she would ask her aunt to put her in the chute. After enjoying the benefits of the machine, Temple decided it would be a good idea to build one for herself back at school. Of course, eyebrows were raised. But after some convincing, she got one of her teacher's approval and began to design a model of the machine. When in college, she used this machine as the subject of her senior thesis, which proved beyond doubt that college students felt more relaxed when they used the machine.

Was the machine a success? Temple Grandin turned this idea into an important scientific paper in which she first proved it relaxed college students. For herself, the machine served as an important tool in keeping her sensory input regulated. Versions of her machine have come out and are widely used all over the world. Even now in her sixties, Temple Grandin (and many others) still uses the squeeze machine! In addition, this invention marked the beginning of her career as an animal scientist.

Work: Sell Your Work, Not Yourself

Dr. Grandin's work ethic is probably one of the most important elements that shaped her career. She speaks passionately about making sure children with ASD use their skills to find meaningful experiences in the world of work. She states that too many people with great potential are sitting on the couch playing video games. She inspires youth to get busy by getting a paper route and starting a dog walking business. Children with ASD need these experiences as much as anyone, probably even more. For Dr. Grandin, work started early in life.

When Temple Grandin was thirteen, her mother secured a part time job for her at a local seamstress' shop. Her tasks included hand-hemming dresses and taking garments apart. Work was something new. She had not been taught vocational skills in school at this point, but thanks to her mother's encouragement and training, Temple found great success working during this time. The best part was the money she earned! She continued to develop her entrepreneur skills by starting a sign painting business. She hand-painted signs for local businesses. This skill continued in graduate school where she painted signs for the Arizona state fair. The sign-painting business was also a great success. Temple gained new business by developing her portfolio, something to this day she still encourages students to do. Temple carried a notebook of meticulously designed sketches of the signs she created. Today's students can use their iPhones to carry their portfolio.

Dr. Grandin places great emphasis on creating and maintaining a neat, clean, and organized portfolio. For those people with ASD, it may be difficult to walk into a job interview and engage in comfortable conversation. Therefore, Dr. Grandin states, "Sell your work, not yourself." That is what she did. From selling her signs, to selling designs to the cattle industry, Dr. Grandin let her work speak for itself.

At fifteen years of age, Temple went to work on her aunt's ranch in Arizona. She cleaned stalls and did chores around the ranch. (Her love of horses continued at home. Throughout her high school years, she would also work in the horse barn at her school.) At her aunt's ranch Temple would engage in strenuous work that seemed to help reduce the panic attacks to which she was prone. Fixing fences,

"One of the things I figured out is that I had to sell my work and not my personality. I avoided job interviews and I showed prospective clients a portfolio of my drawings and photos of completed livestock handling facilities. Many people thought I was weird but they respected me when they saw my design drawings. Many people make the mistake of putting too much stuff in their portfolio. It is best to put relatively few examples of the very best work. In my book, *Developing Talents*, I provide a lot more tips for making portfolios."—Temple Grandin[b]

riding horses, and replacing a roof all were part of Temple Grandin's daily routines.

Higher Education Leads to Her Career

After she graduated from Franklin Pierce College in 1970, Temple went on to Arizona State University to work on a master's degree in animal science. Based on her experiences with the squeeze machine, she wanted to further understand the behavior of cattle in different types of chutes. Her fieldwork proved difficult because during this time, ranchers actually had a policy that no women were allowed in the feed yards (a place where cattle go when they are ready to be sold). Because she was denied access, her motivation to get inside got even stronger. Temple is famous for saying, "When a door opens you walk through it"; this door was one that was closed, so she opened it herself. Upon being declined entrance into the yard, she went straight to the *Arizona Farmer Ranchman* office and told the editor she was going to write a column for it every week. She got the job. Temple had written an article for the magazine in the past in which she described the differences in cattle chutes. Her writing on cattle chutes opened the eyes of many ranchers—that something so familiar in the ranch could affect the health of an entire cattle herd.

Now she had a press pass. No one could bar her entrance into the feed yards anymore. That doesn't mean she had it easy. Most people still were not nice to her; they didn't want her there, much less telling them how to do things at their feedlots. Some went as far as to cover her car with bulls' testicles! That didn't stop her. She was back to the yard the very next day. Despite the resistance from ranchers, many others saw the value of her writings. Here, for the first time, someone was talking about cattle as sentient beings and not just a product. From some ranchers' point of view, it made sense that the better the animals were treated, the better the final product.

She observed that some of the chutes actually hurt the cattle. If the meat is bruised, it cannot be sold for human consumption, so that was just bad business for ranchers. Injured or frightened animals don't put on weight as fast as happy animals, so it made sense to do everything possible to keep them happy. Her observations helped the ranchers make a better profit. They were on board for that!

Keeping the cattle from harm was one thing; keeping them calm and free from fear was another equally important concept. Ranchers often used electric prods to get the herd to move. Temple saw that a rancher's jacket hanging on a post and flapping in the wind would spook the cattle as they walked by, forcing ranchers to prod them through. But when she moved the jacket out of sight, the cattle would walk through no problem. Other details that the ranchers missed, like hanging equipment or shadows, had the same effect. Temple proved how simple fixes could increase the efficiency of the movement of cattle.

Her articles became popular reading for ranchers, and she was even asked to contribute a chapter to a book on feedlot design. After receiving her master's degree, she secured many clients who wanted her consultation services. She continued to write articles and also worked part time for a company that built cattle feedlots.

Temple Grandin's career took a major step forward during a visit to a livestock show. At the time ranchers in Arizona were concerned with an outbreak of scabies within the cattle population. Scabies is a contagious disease spread by mites. They lay their eggs under the skin of the cattle, who then develop terrible itching that spreads throughout their bodies. Cattle scratch so hard they lose hair, develop infections, and can even die. The only way to battle the infestation was to dip each animal in a vat of pesticide that killed off the mites. But these vats were causing terrible problems. The cattle refused to walk into the vat of liquid (even though cattle are good swimmers). In fact, it was so bad that some would jump and flip themselves over and drown in the liquid. No one could figure out what was frightening the cattle.

Temple was asked by a rancher to figure out what was going wrong. She immediately went to visit a dip vat and sort out the issue. She was able to figure out what no rancher could. The cattle were being frightened by the metal ramp that led into the bath. It was slippery and made the cattle feel as if they were falling, not walking. She designed a new dip vat that had a gentler slope, a concrete path to walk on, and created a steep drop off (the cattle had to be submerged over their heads for the pesticide to kill off all the mites). The steep drop-off meant the animal would quickly drop into the vat, go under, and rise back up quickly before it could be afraid. There were other advantages to Temple's design, which would easily and efficiently move the herd through the vat, dry them off, and move them back into the yard.

After the design was finished and the new dip vat built, it was tested. Unfortunately, it didn't work. Two cattle drowned on the first day. What went wrong? Temple was positive her design would work. She quickly visited the plant to figure out what went wrong. And then she saw the problem. Against her design, the rancher covered the concrete path with the slippery metal that made the animals feel if as they were falling. The metal was removed, and the new system worked perfectly. Cattle willingly entered the dip vat and moved through with ease. Now the process was without fear and even enjoyable for the cattle. Word of her design spread all over the world. People were clamoring to get her to help solve problems and develop new ways of managing cattle.

In 1975 she was hired to design a new handling facility from the ground up. She designed a system to manage the cattle that not only met their basic food and water needs, but met their emotional needs as well. Her design complimented the fact that cattle like to walk single file in a curved path. In her facility the cattle cannot see anything that might frighten them. As you might imagine, the floors are not metal, but rather have a surface that is easy for cattle to walk on.

Temple Grandin has made major improvements in the processing of cattle in this country. She has found a way to humanely slaughter animals so that they feel no pain nor fear as they move through the system. After observing some terribly inhumane methods of slaughter, she sought to change such behavior and has had great success. Temple Grandin even gave up eating steak early in her career after seeing these horrible methods and cruel ways of treating cattle. She even states,

Advice from Temple Grandin

The following tips about developing good work skills come from Temple Grandin's article titled "Keys to Successful Living, Employment and a Good Social Life for Individuals with Autism and Asperger's":

Develop Good Work Skills: This tip applies to individuals on both the high and low ends of the spectrum. The most basic skill is getting to work on time. When I was little I was taught this skill because I was expected to be ready at 7:30 so I would not be late for school. When I was 13 I had a sewing job two afternoons a week. In college I interned during the summer at a research lab and at a school for children with autism. I learned valuable work skills. I also had to learn that much of the work was interesting, but there was also boring work that had to be done. When I was starting my design business, it took three years to learn cattle handling and facility design. Even though I had the innate ability of visual thinking, I had to work hard to develop my ability into a design business. Below are some tips to help you keep your job.

- Never tell other people that they are stupid even if they are stupid.
- Do not tell dirty jokes or express your opinions on politics or religion at work.
- You have to do things that your boss tells you to do.
- Do not go over your boss' head unless a major project is going to fail or your job is at risk.
- Freelance work is often easier because office politics is avoided.
- Ask for directions in writing so you do not have to remember long strings of verbal information. A good way to do this is to tell your boss that e-mail is a preferred method of communication.
- Avoid jobs that require multi-tasking such as cashier in a busy restaurant or a receptionist that has to answer phones and work at a computer at the same time.
- Ask for instructions that are not vague. Some examples of vague instructions are: develop some new software or clean-up the store. Some examples of clear instructions that are easy to understand with a clear goal and endpoint are: "Revise our computer program for handling client contacts so it will be easier to read on a small mobile telephone screen" or "Restock the cosmetic section shelves and pick-up the trash in the parking lot."
- Do not be a pest. When I was six, I was taught not to "wear out my welcome" by going over to a next door neighbor's house too often. At work, do not send 10 e-mails or leave 10 telephone messages to the same person in one day. Do not pester your boss throughout the day. Schedule a time each day to receive directions.[c]

"If I had my druthers, people would have evolved as plant eaters and wouldn't kill animals for food at all. But I don't see the whole human race converting to vegetarianism anytime soon."[4] Thanks to Dr. Grandin there is a system in place that treats animals with greater humanity. Until people evolve to a plant-based species, Dr. Grandin has eased the suffering for millions of animals.

Daniel Tammet

Pi is an amazing number. It is the relationship of a circle's circumference to its diameter. In other words, if you measure the diameter of a circle, its circumference will always be the diameter times 3.14, which is how we usually represent pi. But the truth is pi is an irrational number. It goes on forever with no seeming pattern or end. In fact, scientists have measured pi to about five trillion digits thus far and are constantly working on more.[5] While we have learned pi as 3.14, it is really 3.1456265359 . . . and goes on forever.

In 2010, Daniel Tammet stood in front of a group of mathematicians and began to recite the numbers of pi. He successfully recited the first 22,514 digits. This feat took him just over five hours to complete. He ended not because of any mistake; he just decided that was enough. Armed only with a few bananas, water, and an amazing mind, he showed a skill that only about fifty people in the world have.

Daniel Tammet is a man with ASD who is a savant. He was diagnosed with Asperger's syndrome and has described himself as a high-functioning autistic savant. He is the author of three incredible and insightful books about his experiences growing up and living with ASD. He has also written many articles and translations of other books. In addition, he launched an online site for language courses. Daniel Tammet is active in raising funds for organizations dedicated to studying epilepsy and ASD. He has given us a look into his incredible abilities and is the subject of many scientific studies to understand how his brain works. Daniel's gift for numbers and language is astounding. He readily calculates complex mathematical equations in his head. What makes him most unique is his ability to explain how he does his lighting-speed calculations, and how he memorizes such vast quantities of information.

Born in England in 1979, Daniel is the eldest of nine children. As a baby he was difficult to comfort. His parents reported that his only comfort was food and motion. At times when Daniel was an infant, his father would need to rock Daniel as he fed him in order to sooth him. Daniel's crying was relentless, and his parents needed to work around his outbursts. Doctors could find nothing wrong with him, and his excessive crying continued. (It should be noted that excessive crying in babies is often a sign of future problems such as attentional difficulties and

Daniel Tammet has given the world great insight into ASD. *Photo reprinted courtesy of Jerome Tabet*

behavioral problems. Excessive crying, or colic, is now believed to be neurological with a hypersensitivity to stimulation and sensory overload.) Daniel's development in other areas seemed normal. He walked and talked at the age of one. But his behavior did not improve. He was prone to banging his head on a particular wall in the house. He would rock for long periods of time, slap himself so hard as to produce bruises while screaming at the top of his lungs, and frequently throw tantrums.

As a toddler he entered nursery school. His earliest memories were those of the tactile surfaces of floors and materials in the room. He reported having no memories of other children because to him they were all background noise to his visual and tactile experiences. He did not engage with others; instead he spent the time walking barefoot and repeatedly enjoyed the experience of having his foot stick to a plastic mat, finding comfort in the sticking sensation on the soles of his feet. Watching spinning coins and moving toys back and forth were other enjoyments. As you have read thus far, these behaviors are relatively common amongst the ASD population.

In his book *Born on a Blue Day*, Daniel writes about an important event in his childhood:

> On one of my father's walks down the street with me in the buggy, I called out as we passed a shop window He was reluctant to take me inside. Normally when my parents were out they never took me inside a shop, because on the few occasions they had done so in the past I had burst into tears and had a tantrum. Each time they had had to make their apologies, "He's very sensitive," they would explain, and leave in a hurry. This time my cry seemed different, determined. As my father took me inside he noticed the large display of Mr. Men books. There was the bright yellow shape of Mr. Happy and the purple triangle of Mr. Rush. He took one and gave it to me. I wouldn't let go of it so he bought it. The next day we walked past the same shop and I called out again. My father went inside and bought another Mr. Men book. This soon became a matter of routine, until he had bought me every character in the series.
>
> My Mr. Men books and I soon became inseparable. I wouldn't leave the house without one. I spent hours in the evenings lying on the floor with the books in my hands, looking at the colours and shapes in the illustrations. My parents were happy to leave me to my obsession with the Mr. Men characters. For the first time I seemed happy and peaceful. It also proved a useful way of encouraging better behaviour. If I could go a whole day without having a tantrum they would promise to buy me a new Mr. Men book.[6]

His initial love of books did not include the reading of them. Rather he loved the page numbers printed on the bottom of each page. He stacked the family library in his room, creating a fortress of books. As he learned to read, Daniel would stack categories of books in his bedroom, giving order and structure to this fortress. For Daniel Tammet, his room was his happiest memory. He would stay there for hours, organizing books and enjoying the quiet and solitude.

As you can imagine, school was often difficult for Daniel. He was often picked on and teased; however, his lack of emotional connection to his classmates was often a buffer. Since Daniel generally ignored the teasing, students often gave up and moved on. Despite his lack of emotional connection to others in his class, he longed for friendship. He writes,

> Some of the boys in the playground would come up to me and tease me by mimicking my hand flapping and calling me names. I did not like it when they came up very close to me and I could feel their breath on my skin. Then I would sit down on the hard, concrete ground and put my hands on my ears and wait for them to go away. When I felt very stressed I counted the powers of two, like this: 2, 4, 8, 16, 32 . . . 1024, 2048, 4096, 8192 . . . 131072, 262144 . . . 1048576. The numbers formed visual patterns in my head that reassured me. Since I was so different, the boys weren't entirely sure how to tease me and soon tired of it when I did not react as they wanted me to, by crying or running away. The name-calling continued, but I learned to ignore it and it did not bother me too much.
>
> People with Asperger's syndrome do want to make friends, but find it very difficult to do so. The keen sense of isolation was something I felt very deeply and was very painful for me. As a way of compensating for the lack of friends, I created my own to accompany me on my walks around the trees in the playground.[7]

Talking to himself and walking with imaginary friends helped the hours pass at school. Given his proclivity for numbers, he reveled in seeing patterns and calculations in his head. Late in elementary school he did make his first friend. This relationship would open doors to future relationships, friends, and experiences.

As he got older Daniel was able to build friendships although it required work. He took a volunteer position in Lithuania teaching English. Upon his return to England he developed software for language courses. Daniel's fascination with words and language has led him to learn approximately ten languages himself, and he has even created his own language called Manti. His amazing language and number skills gained much attention and got him a spot on the *Late Show with David Letterman*. When David Letterman asked what abilities Daniel has that others don't, Daniel asked Mr. Letterman his birthdate and was able to tell him what day of the week he was born on. In fact, Daniel Tammet can tell you any day of the week that any date fell on or will fall on—past, present, or future—for thousands of years. He does so by running sophisticated calculations in his head almost instantaneously.

Most fascinating about Daniel Tammet is the fact that he has synesthesia. When he calculates numbers or hears words, he automatically sees a picture or mental representation of the word or number. Early in his life he suffered from epileptic seizures, which he cites as the beginning of his synesthesia. For example, to Daniel the number one is a flash of white light.

Born on a Blue Day

The following extract from Daniel's book *Born on a Blue Day* illustrates his experiences with synesthesia and his love of mathematics:

Scientists call my visual, emotional experience of numbers synesthesia, a rare neurological mixing of the senses, which most commonly results in the ability to see alphabetical letters and/or numbers in colour. Mine is an unusual and complex type, through which I see numbers as shapes, colours, textures and motions. The number one, for example, is a brilliant and bright white, like someone shining a torch beam into my eyes. Five is a clap of thunder or the sound of waves crashing against rocks. Thirty-seven is lumpy like porridge, while eighty-nine reminds me of falling snow. Using my own synesthetic experiences since early childhood, I have grown up with the ability to handle and calculate huge numbers in my head without any conscious effort, just like the Raymond Babbitt character. In fact, this is a talent common to several other real-life savants (sometimes referred to as "lightning calculators"). . . .

My favorite kind of calculation is power multiplication, which means multiplying a number by itself a specified number of times. Multiplying a number by itself is called squaring; for example, the square of 72 is 72 x 72 = 5,184. Squares are always symmetrical shapes in my mind, which makes them especially beautiful to me.

Multiplying the same number three times over is called cubing or "raising" to the third power. The cube or third power of 51 is equivalent to 51 x 51 x 51 = 132,651. I see each result of a power multiplication as a distinctive visual pattern in my head. As the sums and their results grow, so the mental shapes and colours I experience become increasingly more complex. I see thirty-seven's fifth power 37 x 37 x 37 x 37 x 37 = 69,343,957—as a large circle composed of smaller circles running clockwise from the top round.[d]

On Seeing Pi

In describing his ability to remember over twenty-two thousand digits of pi, Daniel describes an ever unfolding landscape of colors and textures. The size of each segment he visualizes varies depending on the digit. Digits can be bright or dark, blended or stand alone.

This is how I "see" the first twenty digits of pi:

The number slopes upwards, then darkens and becomes bumpy in the middle before curving and meandering down.

And here are the first 100 digits of pi as I see them.

At the end of each segment of numbers, the landscape changes and new shapes, colors and textures appear. This process continues on and on, for as long as the sequence of digits that I am recalling.

The most famous sequence of numbers in pi is the 'Feynman point', which comprises the 762nd through 767th decimal places of pi: ". . . 999999 . . ." it is named after the physicist Richard Feynman for his remark that he would like to memorize the digits of pi as far as that point so that when reciting them, he would be able to finish with ". . . nine, nine, nine, nine, nine, nine, and so on." The Feynman point is visually very beautiful to me; I see it as a deep, thick rim of dark blue light.[e]

Daniel Tammet received attention from the public after a documentary called *Brainman* was produced. In this documentary, Daniel and several other savants were featured. Daniel was challenged by the producers to visit Iceland and learn the language. Given Daniel's extraordinary language abilities, they thought that it would be interesting to watch him learn and master the language not in a few years, but in a few days. The Icelandic language is one of the most difficult languages in the world. Its heavy reliance on consonants and many variations of a single word make it difficult for a nonnative to learn. For example, the numbers one through four have three gender forms—male, female, and neutral; thus, the numbers have three variations depending on how you use them. Nevertheless, in seven days Daniel appeared on Icelandic television for several interviews conducted completely in Icelandic!

Needless to say, scientists have been eagerly studying Daniel's abilities. At the University of Cambridge, they looked into Daniel's brain using fMRI. They found no difference in brain structure or the presence of high intellectual abilities as the cause for his extraordinary memory. In other studies,[8] scientists concluded that his abilities may be explained by a hyperactive region in the prefrontal cortex. In any case, Daniel Tammet believes that the combination of ASD and synesthesia is the reason he can calculate and memorize at such amazing speed and depth. The concrete representations of numbers and words form a mental picture that he instinctually commits to memory.

Kim Peek

If you have seen the movie *Rain Man*, you probably know a little about Kim Peek. The famous movie was loosely based on Mr. Peek's life and amazing talents. While Mr. Peek had many of the classic ASD behaviors, such as social withdrawal and delayed milestones, his diagnosis would be better described through his medical condition. While the movie portrays him with ASD, his true diagnosis was FG syndrome, a rare genetic syndrome that is linked to low muscle tone and an abnormally large head.

Kim Peek was born in Utah in 1951. He was born with macrocephaly, which is an enlargement of the head and brain. In addition, Mr. Peek was born without a corpus callosum, which is the bundle of nerve fibers connecting the right and left hemispheres of the brain. He also had damage to the cerebellum, the area that controls many aspects of motor coordination. As an infant his outlook was bleak, according to the doctors. They diagnosed him with mental retardation and suggested he be put in an institution to live out his days. The doctors believed there was no hope of intellectual growth. At the age of six the doctors even suggested that he have a lobotomy to cure his persistent talking.

This amazing story starts with Kim Peek's parents, who were committed to raising him and giving him the best possible life. This would be a lifelong career for both parents. Throughout Kim's lifetime (1951–2009), he needed the constant care of his family. But early on his parents noticed something remarkable. Between the ages of one and two, Kim Peek began to read. Not just read, but memorize the book he read. In addition, he read with remarkable speed. Later in his life it was discovered that Mr. Peek would read the left page of a book with the left eye and the right page of the book with his right eye, at the same time! He would scan a page in about ten seconds while committing it to memory. Interviews reported that Mr. Peek committed about ten to twelve thousand books to memory.

School did not go well for Kim Peek. He was kicked out on the first day he attended. School administration deemed Kim "uncontrollable" due to his continuous chatter, pacing, and fidgeting. Instead of going to school, Mr. Peek had tutors come to the home to work with him. He was done with the high school curriculum at the age of fourteen. When he was eighteen he got his first job working out the payroll at a local community center with 160 people. He never used a calculator nor did he write anything down. This job took him only a few hours a week. He was replaced after a few years by two full-time accountants and a computer.[9] For fun, Mr. Peek would memorize names and exercise his brain by adding up all the numbers in the telephone book, often counting up into the trillions! He also memorized every zip code and area code in the United States, as well as every television station that serves each city.

This amazing ability to read and retain was not limited to books; he could also remember every note an orchestra played. His amazing memory was a problem at times. When his father brought him to a concert, Kim Peek would stand up and yell to the musicians in the middle of the performance that they played the wrong note. He would often correct actors on stage if they got a word wrong during a play.

His gifts were probably a result of the fact that he did not have a corpus callosum. Thus, the brain needed to figure out new pathways between the left and

"Known as 'Kimputer' to many, his knowledge-library includes World and American History, People and Leaders, Geography (roads and highways in U.S. and Canada), Professional Sports (baseball, basketball, football, Kentucky Derby winners etc.), the Space Program, Movies and movie themes, Actors and Actresses, the Bible, Mormon Church Doctrine and History, Calendar Calculations (including a person's day of birth, present year's birthday, and the year and the date the person will turn 65 years old so he or she can retire), Literature/Authors, Shakespeare, Telephone Area Codes, major ZIP Codes, all TV stations and their markets. He can also describe the highways that go to a person's small town, the county, area code and ZIP code, television stations available in the town, who the person's pay their telephone bill to, and describe any historical events that may have occurred in their area."—Fran Peek in *The Real Rain Man: Kim Peek*[f] right hemisphere. The new pathways probably caused a rerouting of information directly into storage areas. Given that he had a larger brain than most, there was more room for information.[10]

Mr. Peek's memory brought him into the public spotlight. He gave lectures and talks and invited the audience to ask him questions about certain historical facts. He always amazed his audiences as he rallied through the entire list of British monarchs and their birthdays. Like Daniel Tammet (the two met several times), Kim Peek could calculate the day of the week a person was born on and tell the person what items were in the newspaper on the day of his or her birth. Mr. Peek had the most developed memory anyone had ever seen. For this he was often called a "megasavant."

In 1984 Mr. Peek met Barry Morrow, who wrote the movie *Rain Man.* Morrow had heard about Mr. Peek and his amazing brain and desired to meet him. At a conference for individuals with disabilities, the two met. Morrow could not get Peek out of his mind, and the movie was soon to come. When actor Dustin Hoffman was chosen to play Kim Peek, his father commented that it was the beginning of the rise of his son's self-esteem. Kim Peek received great attention from the public and began to be invited to give lectures. When Morrow won the Oscar for his work on *Rain Man,* he gave the statue to Kim Peek. The statue is often referred to as the most loved statue in the world. When Kim spoke and lectured, he brought the statue with him. It was inevitably hugged by his many fans.

Kim Peek could never take care of himself, yet had one of the most remarkable minds in history. Thanks to Mr. Peek we have gained tremendous insight into the working nature of the brain and the capacity it has. In addition, as he became more of a public figure, people got a sense of the warmth of his personality. Sadly,

"Audiences clamoured to hear him answer questions off the top of his head, such as who was the game winning pitcher of game three of the 1926 World Series (Grover Cleveland Alexander of the Cardinals). They were stunned by his ability to rattle off facts in about 15 different subjects, including history, literature, sport and the British monarchy. . . . He knew phone books by heart, and could tell you what day of the week a particular date fell upon going back decades. One of his party tricks was to tell strangers the names of the people who used to live next door to them years ago."—Ed Pilkington, speaking of Kim Peek in the *Guardian*[9]

Mr. Peek died in 2009 of a heart attack. He will always be one of the most influential people in the study of the human potential.

Susan Boyle

People live in the world of reality television in which they peer into the lives of others, perhaps to make themselves feel better. The highest ratings for these shows come when someone is subject to some bizarre torment or ridicule. After years of *American Idol*, the only thing remembered is those folks who embarrass themselves for the amusement of millions.

Susan Boyle did the opposite. On her appearance on *Britain's Got Talent*, a show that brings in the general public in a talent show–type program, she destroyed the notion that she would only be remembered for her failure. Skeptically, the audience and judges looked at her and thought they were about to hear someone with no talent. They based this on her appearance. Instead, she is remembered and lauded today as one of the best singers in the world. If you are not one of the ten million people who have revisited the YouTube site on which her performance is posted, you should be.

Susan Boyle was diagnosed with ASD later in her life, but her beginnings were filled with struggle. Born in 1961, she was briefly deprived of oxygen during her birth. As a result, she suffered from learning disabilities in school and was teased because of her struggles. Later, in 2012, she was diagnosed with Asperger's syndrome and was told she had an above-average IQ!

Boyle has been described as eccentric all of her life, often suffering from mood swings and tantrums. Often her mood is affected by the place she is in; thus, she will leave before an explosion happens. She also suffers from depression at times and needs to spend time alone. She admits having difficulty with eye contact and terrible anxiety in new situations.

Fortunately for Susan Boyle, whose debut albums sold over nine million copies, her anxiety and mood swings do not exist when she is on stage. She performs

> "It's a very difficult subject to talk about because you always feel that eyes are on you, and people view you as different. I like to see myself as someone with a problem, but one I can solve. It is definitely getting better. Since the diagnosis I've learned strategies for coping with it and the best one is always to just walk away."—Susan Boyle[h]

show after show with great comfort and ease. She has traveled the world, and every performance goes on with no problem. It is only when she is offstage that she suffers from the anxiety and mood swings.

For Susan Boyle, interviews and basic daily tasks may be tough. Fortunately, she has managers and aides to assist her and help manage the difficulties she may face.

8

PARENTS AND SIBLINGS—WHAT ARE THEIR EXPERIENCES?

To understand what it is like to raise a child with autism spectrum disorder, readers need to hear from people who have had the experience. All the good times and struggles are experienced by each parent in different ways. Parents raising children with ASD have stories to tell that can serve as valuable lessons for all people. For example, the story about Noa and Emma (see page 47) reminds us about the great diversity among people with ASD. It also reminds us of how parents might look to the future and begin to worry. All parents want the best for their children and to protect them from the harshness of the world. Noa and Emma's mom, Maria, discusses the fact that she is constantly looking toward the future, but at the same time has traded control for acceptance. This balance requires great skill and planning. A parent with a child with ASD is constantly thinking about today and tomorrow, planning for the day and the future. In Maria's story we also see that a parent with two children with ASD requires strength.

Raising Two Girls with Autism

Maria is the mother of Emma and Noa, two girls with ASD. She describes her experiences as a parent. What does it take? How does a parent with ASD children think differently from other parents? Maria explains:

Developing, navigating and maintaining relationships are complex enough without throwing autism into the mix. Making connections, expressing your thoughts verbally, engaging in meaningful friendships is a huge struggle for both of my daughters. Watching your autistic child either struggle with or show no interest in making friends makes me feel helpless. This also puts me in the position of having to figure out where they fit in or what their lives will look like in the future, if they are unable to create or seek positive meaningful friendships with others. It makes me ask those painful questions: how will they survive without me in the future? For now, I am their protector, advocate, and of course their mother but my aspirations for them are the same as any other parent raising neurotypical children. I want them to be happy, healthy, and productive. However, there are all those decisions parents make that involve schools, religion, neighborhoods, and doctors while they are raising their children. Certainly, there are life choices these children will have to make for themselves as young adults: what college they want to attend, if and who they want to marry and if they want to have children. These parents of neurotypical children plan and save for their children's college fund or a possible wedding and the prospects of maybe someday they'll get to be grandparents. But these choices are not in the cards for me and my daughters. I'll be making decisions for my children from birth to well past their eighteenth birthday like choosing a lawyer for estate planning, applying for legal guardianship and asking family and friends if they would be willing to be their legal guardians if something happens to me and my husband (and the feeling that comes with asking: you never want your kids to be a burden to anyone), talking to professionals about SSI [Supplemental Security Income] and other programs after the girls turn twenty-one. The thought of what will become of my daughters once I leave this earth is the most frightening and painful thought. Who will be their protector, advocate? Certainly no one will be their mother, no one will love them more than me, no one.

As a parent with special needs kids, every now and then I get to peek into the world of a parent with worries that can't compare to mine. But I often find myself listening to a close friend constantly complaining about her two neurotypical daughters. And it's not that she doesn't have a right to complain about her life from time to time, but her life as a mother is so much different from mine. Our concerns are different. For example, she wants one daughter to decide at the age of ten what her profession should be as an adult. The other daughter has it all figured out, she'll become a veterinarian but that's not enough so my friend will find something to stress over for that kid. For example, she does not want her to choose French as a foreign language even if her daughter wants to learn French. Her reasoning is that it "makes more sense to learn Spanish, what's she going to do with French?" I know her well enough to say that this comes from her own insecurities. It still angers me just the same! She talks to no end about how much stress they cause her on a daily basis and has even stated how "motherhood is overrated." I understand we all have our moments and she's entitled to complain like anyone else. But I can't help to feel a certain way when I hear her grumble about how much they whine and behave like their father. How they lollygag while she's trying to get them out of the house to attend a soccer game. I sometimes want to tell her, Hey! I wish I had your problems! Instead, I just listen for the most part and while I think she's a terrific mother, I have expressed how she would probably fall apart if she had kids with autism. Most of her worries are about the present while mine are about the future. Although life brings many unforeseen surprises and we can't predict anything, my friend has appropriate concerns for her young children's well-being, but it will be short-lived and she'll, no doubt, raise independent, self-sufficient, productive young ladies. And if they don't turn out to be the scholars and professionals she wanted to be, she still gets to dream of a bright future for her daughters. All this brings to mind that well-meaning phrase I've received from people who are trying to make "me" feel better or maybe they don't know what to say: "God only gives you what you can handle." It's not something I subscribe to or makes me feel better but maybe there is some truth to that. I've met some pretty strong parents who are raising children with special needs. I believe that we handle our situation and persevere in the face of adversity, with strength found in the love we have for our children.

Overall, this makes me think about the trade I made over the years as a parent to my daughters. I traded control for acceptance. I gave up trying to control autism and learned to accept my daughters as they are, beautiful. This is turn gave me permission to accept myself as their mother, loving them unconditionally and I will forever be grateful to both of them, my teachers, for loving me unconditionally. I try not to let the challenges of raising my girls and living with autism get in the way of having them live their lives to the fullest potential. And my biggest desires for my girls aren't any different from anyone else who is raising neurotypical teenage children. I wish for them to be safe and respected, happy and healthy, productive and independent. As gifted individuals, I also hope that Noa and Emma continue to express themselves and warm the hearts' of everyone they come in contact with in this world because they have a lot to teach and the world has a lot to learn from our children![a]

Parents are inevitably the experts on their child and their child's needs. Although their experiences may require special adaptations to the daily routines and modifications of day-to-day life, most of the time parents with children with ASD are raising their children like anyone, providing a safe and comfortable environment. But what it takes to accomplish this goal does require some extra work, thinking, planning, and emotional energy. How educators and clinicians work with an individual with ASD relies heavily on the parental experience. Educators must listen to the stories of parents if they plan on providing a successful program. For example, Shalini is the mother of ten-year-old Aaryan, who has ASD (read Shalini's story on page 139). Based on years of experience working with Aaryan, she knows a lot about Aaryan's educational and clinical needs. She knows that sensory regulation is going to take a carefully detailed plan in school. Educators can learn so much about an individual's past and present needs simply by listening.

Parenting and Stress

There is a lot of research about parenting that is important to note. For example, parents who are raising a child with ASD report higher levels of stress than

An Interview with Aaryan's Mother

Shalini is the mother of Aaryan, a ten-year-old boy with ASD. Shalini's words tell us that raising a child with ASD requires everyone's input and a lot of extra energy. With a good plan in place, and the support of his family, Aaryan has found many successes in his young life.

"Too much of anything is never good" is often a good strategy to remember with Aaryan. No matter how much fun he is having with an activity, if he ends up playing for too long, there is a lot of sensory bombardment, novelty going on so it is imperative to give a break. It is often misunderstood that meltdowns happen due to him experiencing something he is not sure about, or he is fearful of, or something he dislikes. The nervous system takes a long time to recover even after he is calm and organized. Aaryan's sensory needs are complex. The demands placed on him certainly adds stress chemicals and when his nervous system is tired and drained, it could trigger a meltdown. It is important to be proactive and lower the stress levels regularly to keep him regulated and out of danger zone.

Q: *What are the daily sensory issues Aaryan faces?*

A: Aaryan seeks visual stimulation on a daily basis. His sensory needs are substantial and can interfere with his daily functioning. We have good days and bad days. Aaryan is unable to regulate his sensory needs and that often leads to overstimulation, thus, putting him in "fight-or-flight" mode. We are teaching him coping skills but at this time, he is not able to use them in the heat of the moment.

Q: *What were the first indicators of ASD? How young was he?*

A: Aaryan didn't have meaningful words at age eighteen months. We took him for a routine eighteen-month checkup to the pediatrician and she recommended an early intervention evaluation. Aaryan was interested in wheels, round objects, washer-dryers, and anything that spun. He didn't sleep through the night until the age of three. He was also a very picky eater. I found it extremely difficult to manage him for the most simple task. But it never in a thousand years occurred to me that he has autism. When he got the diagnosis of PDD-NOS (pervasive developmental disorder—not otherwise specified) at age eighteen months, it was devastating for our family. I knew "time is of the essence" and we had to help him as soon as possible. Aaryan started getting speech therapy and occupational therapy very soon.

Q: *What happens in the home in terms of modifications?*

A: As a family we knew we have a difficult road ahead of us. Aaryan started getting therapies at a very early age and that changed his daily routine. I did some research on Applied Behavior Analysis [ABA] therapy. ABA is a scientifically proven analysis that focuses on the principles of learning and motivation. Aaryan responded well to ABA therapy. He began using one-word and short phrases to communicate, but his speech was so unclear that no one could understand him. We tried using PECS, which stands for Picture Exchange Communication System, during his ABA therapy sessions. It didn't sit very well with me. My motherly instincts were telling me that if we keep pushing him to talk, he would get better. But it was a lot to expect and it required team work. We had a meeting with his speech therapist and we all came to an agreement to discontinue using PECS because Aaryan had the ability and capacity to produce sounds and words. Besides, we were afraid if we used PECS we would never ask or push him to use his words and just depend on pointing. We collaborated with his occupational therapist, speech therapist, and the ABA therapists. It was concluded that with the help of sensory diet, helping Aaryan articulate the short list of words he had would help him be more functional. For our family, we looked at things from a practical standpoint. Aaryan's test results showed his memory was above average. It was a good way to use that to our advantage, in other words, "teach him things that he wouldn't forget." We focus on things he can do rather than things he cannot do. We modify his routine according to his needs which are constantly changing. For our family, Aaryan's needs are a priority but we also make sure to not let his disability get in the way of having a somewhat normal life.

Q: *What happens when you go out or to family functions?*

A: Aaryan does well when he goes out to family functions. We prepare him ahead of time what to expect and take his favorite activities. He recognizes his relatives and family members and is often eager to meet them. Aaryan also travels very well. Last year, I took him to India for two weeks. It was a smooth sail.

Q: *What has been the greatest amount of growth?*

A: We video-taped Aaryan's therapy sessions to see his progress. It is easy to forget how difficult it was for him to produce sounds. We didn't expect him to read, write, and speak in sentences. Aaryan's greatest amount of growth is speech and language.

Q: *What do you provide in home or with an outside agency?*

A: Aaryan has been getting ABA therapy since he was two and a half years old and continues to get ABA at home after school.

Q: *School experiences? What modifications are needed in school?*

A: School can be challenging for Aaryan. There is a lot of sensory bombardment and a lot more demands placed on him. It is difficult for him to comprehend and go through transitions smoothly. By that I mean transitioning from one activity to another, especially if it is a preferred activity to a non-preferred activity. Aaryan's school provides a daily sensory diet that allows him to regulate his nervous system to be able to function in the classroom among his peers. Aaryan's needs are substantial and continuous. The school provides him the learning opportunity and most importantly, the exposure he needs to be around his peers for learning and growth.[b]

those raising children without ASD.[1] That seems obvious. Parents of children with ASD have additional stress just trying to get their child involved in social interactions. They have higher concerns about atypical behavior and outbursts, and additional stress of ensuring effective commination. Other sources of stress for parents include a lack of adequate professional support and social attitudes toward individuals with ASD and a lack of awareness about understanding the

Aaryan and his mom enjoy a day in the park. *Photo reprinted courtesy of Shalini Babbar*

problems they and their families experience.[2] In many cases lack of sleep and lack of "alone" time for the adult, on top of the normal parenting stress that every parent faces, can create a difficult experience for a parent of a child with ASD.

Stress in mothers raising a child with ASD can be quite serious. In a study that measured mothers' hormone levels associated with stress, scientists found that their levels were equal to soldiers in combat.[3] What they measured was a very low hormone level that represents the physical residue of daily stress. Thus, mothers may experience chronic stress. This type of stress has been associated with other physical issues such as glucose regulation, healthy immune functioning, and mental activity.

Where Does the Stress Come From?

Research on mothers supporting children with ASD has highlighted areas in which they feel they need additional help.

Unmet needs reported by mothers	Percent of all mothers
Help with care during holidays	93
To do things parent enjoys	91
Advice on best way to help child	87
Break from caring for child	87
Someone to talk to	85
Advice on child's future education	83
Help plan for child's future	81
Managing child's behavior	80
Advice on which services are available	79
Money	71
Planning for child's future	69
Meeting other parents	69
To enable parent to spend more time with other children	63
To enable parent to spend more time with partner	61
Parent's education, skill, and interests	60
To travel/holiday with child	55
Respite care	55
Child's sleep pattern	52
Transporting child	48
Look after child at family and community events	48
Emergency child care	48
To enable caregiver to get employment	45
Housework	44
Emergency health care	43
Adapting house	39
Finding a school for child	37[c]

Excessive worry about these seemingly typical activities may be a result of the many extra steps one needs to take when meeting any of these needs. For example, during school holidays a teen with ASD may not be able to be at home alone. Parents who work must find alternative care for their child while most other teens can manage for themselves. And what about finding a school? Most parents can enroll their child in a local school. But a child with ASD needs a uniquely tailored program.

Finding a School for Matthew

Andrea is the mother of Matthew, a sixteen-year-old boy who is now in high school. Her story highlights the difficulties and extra effort involved in finding an appropriate school placement. In many cases, parents cannot find a school and must provide that educational environment in the home.

According to Andrea,

The decision to homeschool Matthew was easy. The path that led to that decision and the execution of the program was not. From the time that Matthew's developmental challenges first emerged, we faced waiting lists and rejection at every turn. First we encountered the five-month waiting list to even be evaluated by a developmental pediatrician. Once we received the autism diagnosis, we faced more waiting lists for speech and other services. We were rejected by every school we visited. We then had the opportunity to start a new school for children with autism with a small group of parents and a doctor who was eager to help address the shortage of quality services that existed at the time. We jumped at the chance.

The school was up and running when Matthew was three and a half. I sat in the small dark room behind the two-way mirror and watched as teachers worked one on one with my little boy. Week after week, I tried to fight my fear and sadness as I watched him practice the same material over and over with no apparent progress. I was told to be patient. The school was helping some of the children, but the therapeutic approach used was not working for my son. I kept asking why he seemed to be losing ground rather than advancing, and I was told that this was just what his autism looks like.

As Matthew was nearing his sixth birthday, I kept hearing and reading professional proclamations that if children did not talk by the time they were six years old, they probably never would. I was devastated. The window was closing and my son had no language. I continued to observe him at school as teacher after teacher tried to get him to stop his "autistic" behaviors. As one maladaptive behavior subsided, two more popped up. I watched as teachers constantly requested his attention and cooperation and I could not escape feeling that our attempts at therapy were forcing him to retreat more deeply inside himself. After two years of watching my sweet toddler grow into an angry, rebellious, withdrawn, nonverbal boy, I knew I had to try something different.

At around that time, I learned about the Autism Treatment Center of America and the Son-Rise Program. The program, in a nutshell, teaches parents and others to follow the child—their interests, motivations, and even their maladaptive behaviors—to help connect with the child and help the child grow from that point of connection. The website at the time was a little crunchy for my taste and professionals I consulted about the program mostly just rolled their eyes. I was employed full time and the thought of pulling my son from the school we had helped to start and educating him at home had not been part of my plan. The decision, however, was clear. In spite of the resistance I faced from other parents and professionals, I had to bring my son home and try a different approach.

We converted his bedroom into a classroom. The goal of the space was to make it child friendly while utilizing as few visual distractions as possible. Matthew's sensory system was in constant overload and we needed to make the space as peaceful as possible. We began to hire people who we could train to help us run a Son-Rise program in our home. We installed a two-way mirror and eventually a camera in the room so that when someone other than I was in the room, I could watch that individual with my child and provide additional training and feedback. Matthew was in the room with either myself or another adult seven days a week, eight hours a day. We "joined" Matthew in his "autistic" behaviors as the Son-Rise Program encouraged us to do. The teachers and I experienced tremendous personal growth as we learned to love and accept him exactly as he was while wanting to help him progress. For months, he hardly looked at us or even seemed to notice that we were in the room with him as he happily played in his strange and beautiful way. We rarely left the house because his sensitive system just couldn't handle it. When I had moments of doubt about following this unorthodox approach to "educating" my son, I conjured up the memory of that heartbreaking feeling of watching him at school through the observation window.

Each month, I set specific goals which we measured in every session of every day. Each adult who spent time in the room with Matthew filled out a data sheet at the end of each session which I reviewed at the end of each day and compiled at the end of each week. We met as a team biweekly and shared our observations of Matthew's progress. We measured the duration and frequency of his eye contact and interactive attention span. We kept track of the number of word approximations, then the number of words, and then the length of his phrases as well as the clarity of each word. I determined the next goals based on where progress was made and where it was lagging. We used some homeschool curriculum materials, but mostly we used homemade games that we conceived and constructed based on Matthew's interests and motivations.

We did this program for seven and a half years. I encouraged the teachers who were joining him in his room, including myself, to have patience and to cherish the brief but genuine moments of eye contact over the previously forced response to "look at me." Glance by glance, syllable by syllable, Matthew began to emerge from his private world. He began to express that joy and playfulness that had disappeared years prior. We started taking him on little excursions in the neighborhood to expand his experience and increase his tolerance of sensory stimuli. I enrolled him in outside educational classes where he would still work one on one with a therapist but would at least see other children. When Matthew began to show an interest in his peers, I started to explore the idea of getting him back into a school environment and soon discovered that he still didn't really fit in to any of the schools that served children with autism. He briefly attended the original school, and I was grateful that they tried to accommodate him, but the experience was no more successful the second time around. When we looked at other schools, we faced rejection and refusal all over again.

I then heard from several different sources about a school that serves students with a wide variety of disabilities and not solely students with autism. I went to an open house and visited both the middle and high schools. I fell immediately in love with all aspects of the program and the educators who lead it. I could picture my son thriving and blossoming

Matthew's school experience has had its twists and turn. Fortunately, each experience has added to his joy of life! *Photo by Andrea Pollack*

in this stimulating and nourishing environment that embraced each student's strengths. I was afraid of feeling so passionate about the school, particularly because I could see that my son appeared more challenged than many of the other students. I was confident that he held so much potential but had not yet been able to convince anyone else that was true. I submitted an application and braced myself for the rejection I was certain was coming. The call came. I burst into tears despite having promised myself that I wouldn't. He just started his fourth year at this school and I am deeply grateful that its leaders took a chance on my perfectly imperfect boy with his spark of potential.[d]

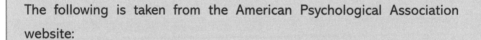

Understanding Chronic Stress

The following is taken from the American Psychological Association website:

Stress is often described as a feeling of being overwhelmed, worried, or run-down. Stress can affect people of all ages, genders, and circumstances and can lead to both physical and psychological health issues. By definition, stress is any uncomfortable "emotional experience accompanied by predictable biochemical, physiological and behavioral changes." Some stress can be beneficial at times, producing a boost that provides the drive and energy to help people get through situations like exams or work deadlines. However, an extreme amount of stress can have health consequences and adversely affect the immune, cardiovascular, neuroendocrine and central nervous systems.

How Stress Harms Your Health

In addition, an extreme amount of stress can take a severe emotional toll. While people can overcome minor episodes of stress by tapping into their body's natural defenses to adapt to changing situations, excessive chronic stress, which is constant and persists over an extended period of time, can be psychologically and physically debilitating.

Unlike everyday stressors, which can be managed with healthy stress management behaviors, untreated chronic stress can result in serious health conditions including anxiety, insomnia, muscle pain, high blood pressure and a weakened immune system. Research shows that stress can contribute to the development of major illnesses, such as heart disease, depression and obesity. Some studies have even suggested that unhealthy chronic stress management, such as overeating "comfort" foods, has contributed to the growing obesity epidemic. Yet, despite its connection to illness, APA's *Stress in America* survey revealed that 33 percent of Americans never discuss ways to manage stress with their healthcare provider.

Chronic stress can occur in response to everyday stressors that are ignored or poorly managed, as well as to exposure to traumatic events. The consequences of chronic stress are serious, particularly as it contributes to anxiety and depression. People who suffer from them are at twice the risk for heart disease than people without these conditions. Additionally, research has shown that there is an association between both acute and chronic stress and a person's abuse of addictive substances.[e]

Despite the Stress . . .

Difficulties having a child with ASD are easy to highlight. The general attitude of people without children with ASD is that parents who are raising children with ASD must have it tough. They must be superheroes or special people to be able to endure what they do. However, most parents of children with ASD do not agree with those statements; in fact, such comments may even be interpreted as insulting. Lisa Smith, parent of two children with special needs (one child with ASD), and writer about ASD states,

> **Parenting a special needs kid does not make you a superhero.** I am not supermom, not even close. I rarely cook anymore. I don't spend enough

one-on-one time with any of the kids. I lose my patience and raise my voice occasionally. I feel really successful on the days I keep the laundry done, the house fairly clean, and the kids happy. . . .

People often say to me, "I don't know how you do it!" or "You are amazing" and "I'd never be able to do the things you do." I always respond with, "I do it because I have to. You would be able to do the same for your child."

I had lunch with a dear friend yesterday. Her son has low functioning autism. He cannot talk. He does not sleep much at night. He is an escape artist and cannot be left alone for even a minute. Some days my friend feels a little sad about it but mostly she does not. Her son is a great kid with a sweet disposition. She tries to concentrate on the things he can do instead of the things he cannot. After hearing some of my friend's latest stories about her son, I heard myself saying, "I don't know how you do it! You are amazing." She responded with, "I do it because I have to. You would be able to do the same for your child." Of course I would.[4]

Along these lines there are definite benefits to the individual who is raising a child with ASD. Lisa Smith goes on to state,

Parenting a special needs kid is rewarding, more so than anything I've ever done. The small things are often huge in our worlds. I had heard it before I had my own special kids: "He has taught me more than I could have possibly taught him." I used to wonder what that could really mean, imagined that I might know; but I did not. I'm not sure anyone could understand without walking in the shoes we walk in. It's life lessons we learn. It's compassion, patience, joy, and empathy on a level that no one could have ever described to me before I became a parent to a special needs child.[5]

Scientific research tends to agree with Lisa Smith. Studies around a concept called stress-related growth show that when parents have the proper resources for their children, the experience results in higher levels of satisfaction and positive views about their experiences. It is similar to the analogy of a tree bending in the wind. A tree bends to the wind and then returns to its upright position, but its trunk is a bit stronger because of the experience. *Proper resources* does not mean financial only; it means that the parent has proper coping mechanisms, proper support systems, and the ability to regulate emotional responses. Parents need the support of family members and friends when raising their children with ASD.[6]

There are other benefits to parents from raising a child with ASD. Studies have shown that raising a child with ASD has a positive effect on the parent's psychological well-being and the quality of life of the family.[7] Raising a child with ASD can unite a family, forging closer bonds between members and creating better communication between all family members. A child with ASD can help the family develop and strengthen each member's coping mechanisms, resiliency, and problem-solving abilities—qualities that are inherent in basic interpersonal skills.

The strengths that come to parents aren't always measurable by scientific methods. Instead they come from watching their children learn and grow and celebrate smaller milestones. Even though many parents with children with ASD

Wendy and Stephen, a Traveling Success!

Wendy describes her son Stephen's skill with independent travel throughout New York City:

Stephen works hard to keep his body calm and he's getting better at conversation. He makes up lots of songs and his favorite author is Dr. Seuss. He's nineteen. He may look like he doesn't know what's going on, but please don't underestimate him. He could be a walking NYC Transit app, complete with interactive travel planning and service updates. Like any young adult, he is happy to share his expertise and proud of the independence it brings him.

Stephen has always loved subways. He has a subway map in his head and has been to nearly every station. Before everyone had iPhones, family members would call him for directions. We knew he could navigate; we just weren't sure he was able to or interested in doing it for himself. That started because of a misunderstanding.

Shortly after he started high school travel training class, our family planned to meet at a local pizza parlor. I would take his younger sister first and Stephen and my husband would join us. As we were leaving, Stephen asked which pizza place and where it was. While this was a little unusual, he often asked unusual questions so I didn't think anything of it. A few minutes later, I looked out the pizza parlor window to see Stephen (safely) cross the street by himself and come join us. When I asked what he was doing there, he looked shocked. "You said to meet you here." "By

Stephen knows the city well. He's been traveling on his own for years. *Photo by Wendy Banner*

yourself?" "Yes," he answered, looking down at me. "I'm big enough." (My husband had no idea Stephen left without him.)

Stephen was right. He knew more about what kids his age did than I had given him credit for, and it was time for him to start acting more like a teenager. From that first walk in the neighborhood to using public transportation all over the city was a natural progression. It was terrifying for me, but it was tremendously empowering for him.

The first step was walking home from school. He would call me on his cell phone upon dismissal, and we would chat for the ten-block trip.

If I couldn't take the call, he could call another adult (good to have an extended network!) and with a little support from school would remember who to call every day. Simple subway trips were next, with phone calls upon exiting the station.

Now, he's progressed to texting when he leaves and again when he gets out of the train. He takes public transportation all over the city (and we don't have to be on the phone with him anymore).

Stephen understands the NYC subway system better than he understands people. The E train will always run local in Manhattan and express in Queens. Stations are always in the same place, even if service changes reroute the trains. That's reassuring. People are unpredictable. It's the human factor that gives me pause. I worry that something will happen to him because he doesn't understand social cues and might look odd. But, I worry about both my kids, my son with autism and my daughter without. I can't keep them from growing up, so the best I can do is to teach them how to be safe. For Stephen, that means that he must "behave appropriately" (safely act like other commuters) to "keep earning" the privilege of independent travel. He is very motivated to keep this privilege.

Stephen has been traveling independently for years and he's never gotten lost on a train. A few times he's headed the wrong way out of the station, but he's been able to solve that problem himself. He knows that Manhattan is a grid and that streets run between avenues so if he hits the wrong one, he turns around. On the rare occasion when he got out of a train and didn't know which way to go, he called me. He didn't get lost; he just forgot the address the first time he went to his piano lesson alone.

There have been a few glitches. He really likes watching subways, so there have been times when he lingered in the station and was late to an appointment. He enjoys transfers too, which might not be the most efficient way to get somewhere (late again). Some of this was boundary-pushing/teenage behavior and some was probably poor executive function/distraction. All have provided opportunities for us to discuss how being on time is a sign of responsibility (and if he can't be responsible, he can't travel independently).

In the past year, Stephen has gotten a lot better at both time management and problem solving. Now he leaves home extra early so he can watch a few trains pass before heading to school. He also devised an alternate route from school to OT [his occupational therapist's office] to go through stations with fewer train lines so he won't get distracted. So far, he's been on time to school and after-school activities pretty consistently.

He's also branched out. He belongs to Liberty Science Center in New Jersey, so he learned how to take the PATH train to the Bergen County Light Rail. When we went together, I couldn't believe how quickly he knew which way to go. I would have to stop and look around for signs to follow. Stephen can't follow the plot of a movie, but he knows exactly how to find his way efficiently. When you want to go to a museum in (or near) a big city, you need his skill set, not mine. I think I'll keep following him. Chances are, if I do, he'll sing me a good song while we go.[f]

worry about travel, individual stories show that a worry can turn into a great success and something that gives a parent a reason for celebration and joy.

Support for Parents and Siblings

What seems to be an important factor in drawing the positive benefits from the experiences of parenting or having a sibling with ASD is support. There are many different kinds of support available to parents and families that seem to make a big difference in their lives. The first is *factual support*. Factual support refers to each family member learning as much as he or she can about ASD. This may not mean becoming an expert in ASD (remember Lisa Smith's statement, "I am an expert on my child"), but it may help to learn as much as you can about ASD. Factual support will lead to making informed decisions about a child with ASD's plans for education, social opportunities, and day-to-day life. Knowing about things like sensory issues, behaviors, learning differences, and social deficits will help families to guide their children to the steps they need to take to enhance these areas.

Another important support system is *self-support*, or the knowledge of stress management and coping mechanisms. To reduce stress, family members must all make sure they have ample time for themselves. Parenting or having a sibling with ASD can be a full-time experience, yet each family member must have time to pursue his or her own activities and interests as well as have time to simply relax. Everyone needs a break from time to time. Another way to encourage self-support is finding someone to talk with. This may include a psychologist or licensed mental health professional. Such professionals can offer help dealing with

Tips on Dealing with an ASD Diagnosis

The following tips are taken from an online article titled "Dealing with a Diagnosis—From a Parent's Perspective."

Appreciate and Accept Your Child

Being diagnosed with ASD doesn't change who your child is, or how you feel about them. Appreciate all the wonderful qualities your child has.

Accept Yourself

This is not the time to pass judgment on yourself as a parent. Many moms and dads say they feel guilt, and blame themselves for their child's diagnosis.

Accept how you feel. Whether you're having a good day, bad day, IT'S OKAY. Give yourself a break.

Educate and Empower Yourself

Read up on research, services and treatments to help quell the anxiety. Speak with other parents.

Act. Don't React.

Be proactive in getting your child help. Studies show that the sooner your child starts treatment, the better, for him, and for you.

You have the power to help your child, right now. There are many simple techniques you can learn to help your children. Once you learn how you can help your child get better, you'll feel more empowered.[9]

the demands of having a family member with ASD as well as processing emotions and feelings about the experience. Having personal time with a licensed clinician can help a person organize his or her own thoughts and feelings and provide a dedicated time for individual support.

Self-support also includes accepting yourself. No doubt family members will make mistakes. Everyone does. But the families with a member who has ASD have to maintain routines and interactions that may be overwhelming. You may react negatively, yell, throw your hands up, or even feel like giving up. But that is normal. You have to accept the notion that you will do your best, and there will be times when you can't do your best. Accept yourself and your limits. Don't blame yourself or feel guilty if life takes the best from you.

Another important type of support is *social support*. This refers to many different types of support available within the ASD community. The easiest way to gain social support is by joining groups or organizations that are dedicated to the ASD community. Groups such as Autism Speaks or the National Autism Association can provide families with a network of other families sharing similar experiences. These organizations offer ways of bringing families together and allow a sharing of information relevant to the child with ASD. By staying aware of these networks you can stay on top of the latest news and information. Websites offer a large array of special topics and research. They also are very easy to contact when you need specific information.

Local support groups also provide great comfort to family members. There are many parent support groups, mother support groups, father support groups, and sibling support groups that offer family members a way of sharing experiences and talking with others who are having similar experiences. The clinical benefits of support groups are well documented and can lead to better coping mechanisms, reduced stress, and a better home environment.[8]

More Than One Child

Parents with more than one child may have to balance their time and energy among children with and without ASD. There are many things a parent can do to help siblings deal with a brother or sister with ASD in positive and productive ways. The first is by providing an open line of communication. In a household with a child with ASD, nothing should be kept a secret. Instead it is important that all family members are kept informed and educated as appropriate about ASD and the ways to manage behavior. Parents should use these discussions as learning opportunities so that the siblings are well informed.

In addition, a child with an ASD sibling needs attention. There has to be time to celebrate the successes of brothers and sisters, and provide experiences that are important to the siblings of a child with ASD. Each individual in the family needs to be recognized for his or her uniqueness and have experiences that relate to him or her alone. While the child with ASD may require more day-to-day management, activities must be budgeted in for all children in the family. Self-esteem can suffer without genuine recognition of individual achievements. This can be accomplished with an ongoing scheduled time or activity that is dedicated for each sibling. A scheduled time provides a "me" time that a sibling can rely on consistently.

Siblings

As you can imagine, siblings of children with ASD also go through experiences that are unique. If your brother or sister needs an extra amount of support, wouldn't that impact your life? It makes sense that siblings of children with ASD may feel like they don't get the same attention or support.

Siblings may feel embarrassment around peers. Without understanding ASD, others may wonder why someone's brother or sister is acting strangely. They may avoid situations like going to the home of someone whose has a sibling with ASD. Having to explain one's sibling to others can be exhausting and even annoying. In public situations, parents may have developed the tools and techniques to manage a child with ASD's behavior, but not so for the sibling. Restaurants or stores can be places where an ASD receives unwarranted attention of others, and in turn

A Brother's Perspective

Eli is the fourteen-year-old brother of Noah (who is seventeen). As with a parent's story, a sibling's perspective can enlighten people about what ASD means in a family. In this case, Eli's remarkable awareness and understanding serves as the model of acceptance not only for his brother but also the world of special needs.

I hate rollercoasters. All the spinning around, and all the blood rushing to your head. And then there is the climb at the beginning and your heart begins to race. And then everything in your body gets all messed up and it always ends in two ways. Having a boatload of fun, or the worst time in your life. I was always in door number two. I had the worst time ever. You could not pay me to go into a rollercoaster.

But Noah does them.

Noah, my brother. A special needs kid is willing to go on rollercoasters more than me, a "normal" person. Noah isn't the guy that says "no," he is the guy that says "yes." Noah is willing to try more things than me. He looks to the possibilities. He is ten times braver than I'll ever be. I could do better to follow his example.

There are things that come easier to me, but bravery is not one of them. Noah has an activity every day after school. Every single day. I have two things after school, and I do them both with him. And just to clarify, he doesn't like to start up fights, or see how much he can get away with. He is brave because he tries everything.

While Noah is my older brother, it doesn't always feel that way. We feel like equals. Noah does require some protection or advice from time to time, but not really anymore. But like most brothers, Noah can be the biggest pest I have ever known. He always pushes my buttons, from right when he gets home from school to before I fall asleep. Not go to bed, mind you; fall asleep. We share a room, so Noah is still running his commentary for a while before we doze off. And Noah knows he does this, because he admits that he likes doing it. I'm not innocent, but it's not like I'm the only troublemaker.

When Noah and I are fighting, it doesn't ever feel like a one-sided fight. He is just as strong, quick-witted, and sane as you or I. Noah has the same drive to win, to accomplish more, that every other person does. So when we are fighting about why he is putting his computer on my desk, or am I taking up too much space in the car, Noah doesn't give in.

But in a weird, twisted way, our banter is how we have fun. Our banter drives Mom and Dad up the walls. It's sort of like the opposite of magnets. If we are both goofing off, or both quiet and restrained, then we get along fine. In this case, opposites do not attract.

Noah and I have our own twisted jokes that nobody really understands, but we get it in our own way. Sometimes we just annoy other people together, or just do it for our own entertainment.

This is going to sound really crazy, but these are the times I feel the closest to him. I can always undoubtedly say that Noah has got my back, which is why I always have his too. I remember one time in fifth grade. My class had a potluck, which is an evening where the entire class and their families gather in one place outside of school and do activities. This particular one was at one of the student's house. Most of us, including Noah and I, were in the basement watching *Family Guy*. But Noah didn't really like *Family Guy*, so he went to go play pinball (yes, they had a pinball machine) in the next room over. Noah closed the door and everything, but we could still faintly hear the pinball machine. Some kids started complaining, and others were yelling to turn it off.

I told everyone to lay off him, and that the noise was really soft. It didn't work. Eventually, one of the kids asked me to tell Noah to turn it off. I was really mad by this. I couldn't think of why they didn't ask Noah to turn it off. What was more, nobody actually went into the room and asked Noah to turn it off, which I thought might be the source of the problem. What was he, a dog that only listens to its master? No, he's not. But I didn't think it would be good for Noah if he was causing commotion like this.

I went into the other room and asked Noah if he would hold on playing for now, as there were only five minutes left in the program. He said yes, easily. I then asked him why he didn't stop when everyone had been telling him through the door. He said that he had not known that they were talking to him, because nobody had said his name. Just what I thought. People have treated Noah like this because he acted differently than other people. But in all the ways that matter, he is just the same as anyone else. I have very occasionally asked myself, if I could change Noah so that he no longer had special needs, would I? I always arrive at the same answer. No. If I did that, then he wouldn't be Noah anymore. It's not like Noah is a bumbling idiot. He is like other people, with strengths and weaknesses. If I changed Noah at all, then he wouldn't be Noah anymore. He is my brother, and I wouldn't have him any other way.[h]

create embarrassment for a sibling. Any child or young adult is concerned with his or her appearance in public. He or she wants to make good impressions on friends. Having a sibling with ASD may, at times, get in the way.

These feelings are absolutely normal. Jealousy about receiving less attention or embarrassment will no doubt be a factor in the life of a sibling (for that matter most siblings, ASD or not, go through these feelings). And like parents one cannot blame him- or herself for feeling this way. Instead it takes time, patience, and adaptations to become immune to the stares of the public. Hopefully, the more educated the public becomes, the more the problem will fade. There are also strategies siblings can use to get through difficult times and modify their feelings.

The sibling of a child with ASD may often become the target of aggressive behavior. After all, living in the house and spending a lot of time together increases the chances for being on the receiving end of a strike. In addition, worrying about the future of a brother or sister can place undue stress on the sibling.

How to Cope

Communication

It takes time for parents to come to terms with a child with ASD; it takes time for them to learn strategies and provide plans that are going to make a difference. For a sibling this may seem like a waiting game or a holding pattern. The first important coping strategy is to make sure a sibling is communicating his feelings to the parents. It is important to let parents know about concerns. Siblings need a place to let others know how they are dealing with a sibling with ASD. Siblings should not feel afraid to ask questions and to seek information from their parents. Appropriate information from parents can reduce the effects of stress. Since anxiety can frequently result from a lack of information, siblings need to understand as much as they can about ASD. Therefore, efforts should be made to educate siblings as much as possible. Younger siblings may think they are going to become like their older sibling with ASD, or older siblings may employ methods of behavioral intervention counter to the needs of a child with ASD. Telling a child with ASD to stop doing something is not always an effective strategy. In some cases, it may make things worse. Therefore, siblings should be involved in all planning and treatment strategies relating to their brother and sister.

Developing a Relationship

All siblings develop relationships. This should be no different if ASD is involved. However, it takes more time and energy to get responses, or reciprocal interactions.

Learning to Interact with Your Brother or Sister with ASD

Go Slow, Think Small Steps

- Remember it takes time to develop relationships, so don't expect things to change overnight. You need to celebrate small breakthroughs and milestones, which may require a lot of patience.
- What are you trying to accomplish? If you want your brother or sister to learn to play baseball, you may be thinking too big. Start with a simple back-and-forth game of catch. Break down large ideas into small steps.
- What you like may not be what your sibling likes. Video games may be too stimulating and drawing may require too much motor control. Find out what interests your sibling has and start there.
- Make sure the language you use is simple and clear. Too much language or talk is not always a good thing.

Be a Role Model

- A sibling is probably the most important role model a child with ASD can have. So you must demonstrate the skill you are trying to teach or the response you are trying to get.
- Your praise will matter. Celebrate a success with praise. Do so every time a successful task is completed.
- Study up on how to prompt and demonstrate using hand-over-hand modeling (see chapter 5).

Get Help When You Need It

- If you need help, ask. There is no shame in not knowing what to do. There are many people who can provide support in the family or community. Seeking help from a counselor is a great way to help manage stress or difficulties related to having a sibling with ASD.

> • Make time for yourself. Don't forgo your own interests and activities. A child with ASD needs special attention, but she don't need you all the time. You need time to develop your own interests.

So for a sibling of a child with ASD it takes more work and education. Techniques found in Applied Behavioral Analysis or Floortime that we have discussed in previous chapters can be employed in daily activities.

In addition to seeking help from others, offering help to others seems to be an effective way of developing coping strategies for the siblings of children with ASD. In a study regarding the coping mechanisms of siblings of children with ASD, it was found that those who were able to help other siblings of individuals with ASD found great relief and benefit in being able to share their techniques. Sharing one's own work with a sibling seems to strengthen his own work and self-esteem.[9]

Another successful technique found in this study was the siblings' ability to redirect the individual with ASD. Simple strategies like verbal prompts, or

The Benefits of Growing Up with a Sister with Autism

Having an autistic sibling means growing up alongside someone who sees the world in a unique, individual way—a way that is often different from the mainstream population. It also means living day to day with someone who behaves somewhat to very differently than the general population. The sibling without autism learns very early on that the world we live in is not black and white; there is not necessarily a right and wrong way to do all things. With solid parental guidance, siblings come to learn that individuality is not scary or wrong, but valued and beneficial to society. The neurotypical siblings go into adult life with open minds and the ability to see the world from many views. Not only does this shape an individual with compassion, empathy, and acceptance of differences, but it also inspires innovation and creativity. The siblings can become real thinkers who see beyond face value.[i]

talking to their siblings about what to expect, deescalated situations that might have ended in tantrums. Using a phrase like "If we stop crying, we can go to the playground," might be the simplest form of managing behavior. However, many siblings found it to be the most effective.

There is no doubt that siblings can have a positive impact. Maureen Angell, Hedda Meadan, and Julia Stoner report, "Previous researchers have found, as we did, that typically developing siblings often help to manage the behavior of and teach their younger siblings with disabilities, modeling appropriate social behaviors and functional skills for them and engaging in prosocial interactions with them. Our sibling participants told us that their parents had taught them some strategies to use to calm or redirect their siblings when needed and that they used positive reinforcement to encourage their siblings to exhibit prosocial behavior. They also directly taught their siblings new skills that helped them function more effectively in social situations."[10]

WHAT SHOULD I SAY?
WHAT SHOULD I DO?

··

The Law

We live in a world full of different cultures, ideas, ways of living, and beliefs. Many of these differences we accept or may not even notice. Our society does a good job of assimilating differences over periods of time, but it doesn't happen overnight. When you think about the trials and struggles of certain communities, you realize the fight for equal treatment happens over many years. The civil rights movement in this country is not terribly old. President Lyndon Johnson only signed this law into effect in 1964. Things that we think should come automatically, like civil rights, actually take the effort of many people to put in place. Even after the law was signed that didn't change many people's opinions or ideas. It takes education and experience to create a society where all people are equal with an equal voice. The same is true for individuals with special needs. The history of equal rights for people with disabilities includes advocacy and struggles that continue in many places in the United States.

In 1954 the U.S. Supreme Court decided the case of *Brown v. the Board of Education*, which set the precedent that every child in the country regardless of race was entitled to an equal education. Specifically, it banned the segregation of African American and Caucasian children in schools. This case brought education into the forefront of politics, and it continued to be a part of the political agenda for decades. In 1975 the Education for all Handicapped Children Act was passed. Prior to this law only one out of five children with special needs received a seat in public schools, with some states even banning children with special needs from general education school.[1] After years of changes and modifications to improve the 1975 Act, the Individuals with Disabilities Education Act (IDEA) was passed in 1990. This law has been updated and modified as recently as 2009. It basically guarantees the right of individuals with a disability to receive a free and appropriate education in the least restrictive environment possible. Like any law, it did not immediately change everyone's opinions or behavior toward the special needs community, but it did bring the situation to the attention of the public and set the stage for equalizing the educational landscape.

Even with a law in place, many parents struggle to find a free and appropriate educational placement for their child with ASD. Attitudes about working with students with special needs may have improved, but there are still struggles. Equal education is important for all to create a climate where those with special needs are truly on equal footing with their typical peers. It starts with our words. What we say and how we say it truly makes a difference.

Language, No One Has Autism

Throughout this book the term "individual with ASD" has been used for good reason. If I say, "He's a blonde," immediately I categorize him into a large group of similarly colored hair people with this certain characteristic. *He*, in this case, is not an individual; he is a category of a type of human beings, blondes. While not overtly offensive, it does reduce the attributes to a singularity I have chosen to highlight. When I say, "He is autistic," I do the same thing. I put him in a category of individuals all sharing a single attribute. In saying, "He has ASD," I fail to recognize the person and highlight the disorder. Person-centered language is always the way to address a description. Whenever we need to highlight a person's attribute, we need to start with the person first—starting with *an individual*, *a child*, *a boy*, *a girl*, *a brother*, *a friend*, and so on defines who the person is first. Thus, he is a person with ASD is the way to go. Saying things like "He suffers from ASD" or "His issue is ASD" is offensive.

Some people disagree with this language. There are those individuals with ASD who prefer to be referred to as an "ASD individual." I have met many people and heard speakers discuss this topic. Their viewpoint is that when we say "individual with ASD," we do indeed recognize the individual first, but we add the ASD, suggesting that the ASD is separate from their individuality.

Lydia Brown writes about this topic in her blog *Autistic Hoya*, and she has clearly given this great thought. As a person with ASD, she is the best source of information. Lydia Brown is an activist, public speaker, and writer focused on violence against multiply marginalized disabled people. Ms. Brown is the co-founder and president of the Washington Metro Disabled Students Collective. She is the author of numerous articles and chapters and is a sought-after public speaker. Ms. Brown is an individual on the autistic spectrum (a term she prefers). She writes,

> But let's think about what we are doing when we use these terms. When we say "person with autism," we say that it is unfortunate and an accident that a person is Autistic. We affirm that the person has value and worth,

and that autism is entirely separate from what gives him or her value and worth. In fact, we are saying that autism is detrimental to value and worth as a person, which is why we separate the condition with the word "with" or "has." Ultimately, what we are saying when we say "person with autism" is that the person would be better off if not Autistic, and that it would have been better if he or she had been born typical. We suppress the individual's identity as an Autistic person because we are saying that autism is something inherently bad like a disease.

Yet, when we say "Autistic person," we recognize, affirm, and validate an individual's identity as an Autistic person. We recognize the value and worth of that individual as an Autistic person—that being Autistic is not a condition absolutely irreconcilable with regarding people as inherently valuable and worth something. We affirm the individual's potential to grow and mature, to overcome challenges and disability, and to live a meaningful life as an Autistic. Ultimately, we are accepting that the individual is different from non-Autistic people—and that's not a tragedy, and we are showing that we are not afraid or ashamed to recognize that difference.[2]

So it should be up to the individual as to how the proper terminology should be structured. But for the many without the voice to express, there are general rules or guidelines. Always acknowledging the individual first is probably best. Of course, times change and terms conjure different meanings with different generations of users.

Personally, at this point in my career, I would never say, "This is a handicapped person." I would say, "This is a person with a disability." *Handicapped* is not a popular term, and of course it is not person centered, but perhaps the term *disability* is also on its way out. Terms like *special needs* are quickly growing in popularity and acceptance. Remember these basics as you construct your terminology. Using terms and phrases that are considerate of the person as a whole are always accepted. Using language that disrespects the person or confines him or her to a single attribute is never a good use of language.

Are Those with ASD Also Retarded?

I can't believe I typed those words "are those with ASD retarded." That question in the world of special needs is never appropriate, and yet it is often a question I am asked by graduate students in the courses I teach at many colleges. I always answer the question with great patience and care. First, the word *retarded* should never be used. Admittedly, in many places it is still used, but the common consensus is that it is just not appropriate. The word *retarded* is exclusive and equates an intellectual disability with a person who is dumb or stupid. Of course this is not the case. A person with an intellectual disability has neurological differences that make certain brain processing work less efficiently or differently than the norm. You know this already, having read this far into the book. Thus, it is your job to correct people when they do use this word.

Having said as much, do individuals with ASD have intellectual deficits or impairments that make their brain processes work differently. Yes. Are they impaired? You know the answer. Sometimes. Learning can be difficult, speech and language processes may be compromised, and how information is stored and retrieved may not be efficient.

"He Seems So Normal."
"She Is High Functioning."

So, what is normal? Do we want the person with ASD to be like us? There is nothing wrong with being a person with ASD, but there is something wrong with an attitude that those with ASD are not "normal." Normal doesn't exist. When you say someone seems normal you suggest that those with ASD are not normal. Like the world, it is the diversity and variability among individuals that is the norm. Saying normal suggests that there is something wrong with the individual. The truth is that those with ASD do have behaviors and problems that might stand out in a crowd. We can choose to accept either all people and their uniqueness or only those we are comfortable with.

High functioning should refer to air conditioners, robots, and power plants. Basically, *functioning* refers to machinery, not people. I will be the first to say, I can't function without my morning coffee. It's a joke that creates the metaphor that I am a car, and without my fuel I can't get moving. It is not a joke to refer to individuals with ASD as mechanical or machine-like, without human virtue. When we think about the incredible sensory and cognitive complexities of individuals with ASD it is the human characteristics that add to their uniqueness. The term functioning is best left to lawn mowers and other appliances.

"I Know Someone with Autism.
You Don't Seem Like Him at All."

At this point I hope you can identify what is wrong with that sentence. "I once knew a person from Argentina. You don't seem like him at all." How ridiculous is that statement? If I said that people would immediately recognize my ignorance

The Reason I Jump

In his book *The Reason I Jump*, thirteen-year-old Naoki answers the question "Would you like to be normal?" Here's what he says:

> What would we do if there was some way that we could be "normal"? Well, I bet people around us, our parents and teachers, would be ecstatic with joy and say, "Hallelujah! We'll change them back to normal right now!" And for all ages I badly wanted to be normal, too. Living with special needs is so depressing and relentless; I used to think it'd be the best thing if I could just live my life like a normal person.
>
> But now, even if somebody developed a medicine to cure autism, I might well choose to stay as I am. Why have I come around to thinking this way?
>
> To give the short version, I've learned that every human being, with or without disabilities, needs to strive to do their best, and by striving for happiness you will arrive at happiness. For us, you see, having autism is normal, so we can't know for sure what your "normal" is even like. But so long as we can learn to love ourselves, I'm not sure how much it matters whether we're normal or autistic.[a]

---

in that I supposed all people from Argentina were the same. Number one, autism is not a "definer." As you have read, the diversity among people with ASD does not allow for a comparison from one person to another.

This sentence also makes it seem like the person to whom the speaker is referring has something wrong with him or her, or that there is something wrong with the person to whom the statement is made. Who compares people anyway? Why would you say, "I know another person your age, and you are nothing like him." You wouldn't, because it makes no sense. Treating people with respect and as individuals is something we all do naturally. This should be no different from the way we treat those with special needs.

"Oh Yeah, I Heard That ASD Is Caused by . . ." or "I Heard ASD Can Be Cured by . . ."

You read this book. You know that there are no consistent markers that can be directly linked to ASD. Even if there were, why would you say that to someone? ASD is not a novelty that deserves off-the-cuff speech. If you were to say to someone with HIV, "I heard that's spread by the transmission of bodily fluid from one person to another," what is your point? There are other ways to show your knowledge and feelings about someone who has a disability or ailment. The best thing to do is be accepting without judgment or without trying to show off your knowledge.

ASD is not something that is "cured," just like being left-handed doesn't need a cure. ASD does not need curing. The hundreds of happy and healthy students with ASD that I have worked with do not need a cure. They need understanding, patience, and a quality educational and therapeutic program.

"I Am So Sorry . . ."

If you meet a parent who says, "I have a son with ASD," you don't respond with, "I am sorry." Parents love their children and are not looking for sympathy. It is condescending to say, "I am sorry," as if the child with ASD has only been a burden and trouble for the parent. It also says that the parent should feel bad. Most parents I know do not feel bad. In fact, they feel quite the opposite. They are optimistic, committed to the welfare of their child, and certainly very involved in the life of their child. Obviously, some things can be awkward to respond to, and chances are the parent has heard it all. Being polite and inquisitive is fine. But we need to know what to say.

Instead of saying "I am sorry," ask questions. Nothing wrong with saying, "That's interesting. How is his school experience?" or "I know a little about ASD. I am interested in learning more." Even asking what his life is like might be okay.

"Wow, Really! Is He Good at Math?"

We don't ask people with ASD if they can do tricks, nor should we be asking about special talents. ASD is not a sideshow. Most people with ASD do not have the savant abilities described in previous chapters. Thus, in many aspects of their lives they develop like most other people. Maybe the individual is average in math (which is most likely). Asking about the outliers, based on the traits we see in movies and the stories we hear on television, shows a lack of knowledge about ASD. And at this point, you know a lot more.

Imagine This Scenario

You are at the doctor's office with your parent. The doctor asks how you are feeling but your parent answers the question. The doctor asks how long you have been feeling this way, again, your parent answers. "For how long?" the doctor wants to know. Your parent answers. What do you say in this situation? When I do it to my daughter, she says, "Dad, let me talk." This is an example of a conversation that pretends you are not in the room.

People with ASD are generally aware of what's happening around them. They are not immune to situations like this. If you have a question for a person with ASD, you should ask. If he or she can answer, then there is no problem. If the person cannot answer, the caregiver can answer instead. The point is that we shouldn't be talking about a person in the room as if he or she doesn't exist. Those with ASD may have difficulty answering, but this doesn't mean we should avoid directing our questions to each individual.

"I Don't Know How You Do It. It Must Be Rough!"

This is something that should never be said to a parent. That statement is less of an acknowledgment of the hard work that it takes to raise a child with ASD and more of a slur. Think about it; when you say this, "I don't know how you do it," it means you could or would never do it ("it" meaning raising a child with ASD). There is also an inference that it is a terrible job that most people wouldn't want. This is untrue. Parents don't ask for accolades or medals for raising their children. Sure, raising any child can be rough at times, but that is small in comparison to the benefits.

"Please Stop Stimming!"

Stimming, as we have discussed, serves a purpose for individuals with ASD. It is a way they can stay calm, think clearly, and feel good. You have to adapt and not give it undue attention. You have to respond as if it is natural. Do not ask someone to stop stimming because it makes you feel embarrassed. Remember, you may stim too. You shake your legs, bite your nails, chew a pencil, scratch, and do many other things that go unnoticed by others. A person with ASD may have stims that do get noticed. So we must be accepting of those behaviors.

"She Looks So Normal!"

At this point you get the message. We have no normal. In addition, ASD does not mean a child looks or acts abnormal. It does not separate them from the rest of the world, and most importantly is does not mean they are not "normal." I recall a parent telling me that a colleague had said about her son, "He looks so normal." To which she replied, "Well, that is insulting. I think he is better than normal."

It is hard to know what to say in any given situation, but hopefully these statements will serve as a reminder of what not to say. More importantly, when you put it all together, you come away with a framework that helps you speak from a place that recognizes that individuals with ASD are unique, wonderful, kind, and special, and just like all of us, they are complex multifaceted human beings.

Social Interactions

In her book *Ten Things Every Child with Autism Wishes You Knew*, Ellen Notbohm writes about the importance of each of us taking responsibility to help people with ASD in their social interactions. The more we know, the more we can help those with ASD to enhance their interactions and engage in activities they may be unable to enter by themselves. It should be the responsibility of all people, when meeting an individual with ASD, to maximize the interaction using our knowledge and a few simple concepts.[3] People need to think about their interactions because it is the general public who must change their behavior to enhance an interaction, not people with ASD.

Among Notbohm's suggestions is the idea of getting rid of the notion that we should fix ASD.[4] I have seen many people meet a person with ASD for the first time, and in an effort to accommodate the individual, they put their face in the direction of the individual's gaze. This often requires a bobbing and weaving of the head to match the gaze of the individual with ASD. As you have read, an individual with ASD may not make eye contact for lots of important reasons. Thus, trying to match the gaze of the individual is trying to "fix" an issue that does not need fixing. If there is no eye contact, do not try and fix that by moving your head into the person's path of sight.

I often see people touch a person with ASD to try and get him to turn toward the speaker or try and gain his attention. This, too, is a situation in which people

How to Talk to an Autistic Adult

The following tips were written by Lydia Brown for her blog *Autistic Hoya*.

1. You are speaking to an adult. Do not use a baby voice.

2. Pause when you're done talking long enough for him, her, or xir to begin speaking or typing. (Xir is a gender neutral pronoun that does not associate with male or female identification.)

3. Be cognizant that the adult may have cognitive processing delays, and give him, her, or xir extra time to process what you're saying and formulate a response.

4. If the adult has a personal assistant, caregiver, parent, or staff person accompanying him, her, or xir, do *not* speak to the Autistic adult through the other person or ask that person questions about the Autistic adult. Address the Autistic adult directly.

5. If you need to ask the adult a question, try to make the question as specific as possible. Broad, generalized, and vague questions are cognitively inaccessible to many Autistic people.

6. Don't stare at the adult if he, she, or xe is stimming—fidgeting with an object or hair, flapping the hands or arms, pacing, making noises, spinning, rocking, etc.—and don't feel awkward about it, either. This is normal and natural behavior. NEVER tell an Autistic adult to have "quiet hands." Ever.

7. If an Autistic adult refers to him, her, or xirself as "autistic," don't correct him, her, or xir and say that that's disrespectful or offensive, and that the adult should be saying "person with autism" instead. Everyone has the right to identify however they wish.[b]

are trying to fix an ASD situation. A person with ASD will stand and face where he or she is most comfortable. So, don't try and fix the situation by moving the person to where you think necessary. On the other hand, a person with ASD may reach out to touch you. He or she may need to do so to judge distance or gain some spacial awareness. It's okay. Don't pull away or move abruptly. You must realize the intent of the person so you don't react in a way that tries to fix the interaction to what you may think is appropriate.

Often a person with ASD may need time to formulate a sentence. Don't try and fix this by finishing the sentence for the person. Give her time to finish the statement; give her time to process and express herself without interrupting.

You may meet people with ASD who stick to one topic. Listen patiently. Don't interrupt and try and change the subject right away. Engage them in their interest before trying to move on to something else. When you do, do so with some care. Don't say, "Okay, enough about *Star Wars*. Let's talk about something else." Having said this, I will say there are plenty of situations in which the interjection of a special interest is inappropriate. I was at a wedding once and sitting next to a person with ASD who only wanted to talk about the number of chairs in the room. During a service it is not okay to talk; thus I was able to politely say, "We can talk about this after the service." During lessons a teacher may tell the student that he or she must remain "on topic" before talking about a special interest.

Don't Take It Personally

If you are on a subway and someone bumps into you, stop and think before you react. I mentioned in a previous chapter about the man who bumped into the woman who became furious and created a situation on the train. The man with ASD did not intentionally bump her, nor was he able to apologize. Those with ASD may walk away in the middle of a conversation, or walk into another person, or do something that may be interpreted as rude. There are opportunities to help an individual navigate those situations, but don't take it personally and get angry or try and correct the person. If one could just tell a person, "Don't do that" and it worked, it would fix the behaviors of ASD. It simply doesn't work that way. In time educators can help those with ASD to correct behavior that is socially difficult, but during an initial interaction you must be patient. Not every interaction with a person with ASD is a learning opportunity. There is a time and place for everything.

There have been plenty of times when I have sat next to students in a cafeteria only to have them say to me, "Can you please not sit here." Well, normally that might be offensive. I always tell our students that they can sit anywhere they like, and they should be welcoming of their peers. However, those with ASD may need that space to be comfortable. I can't say I am never offended (just a little), but I know better than to respond, "Well, that is rude." Instead I will say, "Oh sure, do you need some space?" In this way, I can give the student some language to use that is not seemingly rude. It is our job not to be offended in these situations.

For those with ASD telling the truth may be more important than being polite. I have discussed a difficulty with perspective taking for those with ASD; thus, remember not to be offended if you get the "wrong" answer. For example, you may ask, "Do you like my sweater?" and get a response of "No." You asked. Someone with ASD may not use "little white lies" to protect your feelings. I have often worked with students with ASD who are having trouble with another student. They may be yelling or even hitting another person. When questioned, the response is often "I don't like him [or her]." Most kids may make up an excuse like "He is bothering me" or "She started it." Not so for those with ASD. Concrete and honest is the response.

Inclusive Opportunities

Many people with ASD do seek social isolation or prefer to be on their own for periods of time. So they can't be forced to join in or be part of the group. However, don't assume that all people with ASD don't value friendship. You have read about the communication and social difficulties those with ASD may have. Thus, it is our job to be proactive in including them in social situations. Success will vary, but people need to at least give it a try.

For young children with ASD, parents will often arrange playdates with other children to help begin the process of building friendships. Thus, it is the work of the parents to not only help begin a friendship but maintain it as well. The playdate probably needs some organization to make sure the interaction is maximized. Perhaps the child's favorite toy or snack would be provided at the playdate. Parents may help the children share toys or talk to each other.

For you, as a young adult, it all begins with an introduction, the same way you'd introduce yourself to anyone. Talk about yourself and ask questions about the person's life and interests. The best interactions with people are those in which you can be yourself. Don't be concerned with saying the right thing or doing something wrong. (As Chris, my friend from college, used to say, "Don't be sharp or be flat; be natural.") Get a sense of the person's hobbies and interest in communicating. See what opportunities avail themselves for future interactions.

Most of your initial interactions will revolve around a mutual interest. You are not going to find many students with ASD wanting to sit with the "cool" kids; rather they prefer those who have similar hobbies or talents. There may be tables in the cafeteria that revolve around things like Minecraft, Pokémon, video games,

> ### The Story of Danny
>
> Danny was a sixteen-year-old high school boy with ASD. His passion at recess was playing basketball. However, he would play alone, taking shot after shot on his own. Other students complained that he was taking up the court and interrupting their games. While Danny was interested in shooting the ball, he showed little interest in joining a game or giving up the space.
>
> The school psychologist recommended that the students ask Danny to join and perhaps modify the game. The boys decided that they could play a game called Horse where players take turns shooting baskets. If a player makes it, the next player has to shoot from the same spot. Danny joined, but had difficulty waiting for his turn; thus, he needed the additional support at recess from an adult to help him with the concept of taking turns.
>
> Danny turned out to be the best shooter in the school (probably in the city). No one could match his shots. Quickly he became a sought-after player as the other students tried to match his skills. The game was particularly successful because the rules require imitation. If Danny made a shot from fifteen feet away, the next player had to do the same. In addition, the outburst of screams and encouragement after Danny made a shot turned out to be a great reinforcement for Danny. He enjoyed the triumphant sound of others as the ball went through the hoop.
>
> Over the year, Danny still had a bit of trouble following someone else's shot. If another player got the basket in, Danny usually had to be prompted or shown where he needed to shoot from. However, he welcomed this prompting and followed the directions of the other players. Thus, the interactions were positive and helped Danny to become a part of the basketball community, well respected and admired for his talents.

or other popular games. These are most attractive to those with ASD who want to interact with others.

What You Should Say

I was reminded of a conversation between a principal and a student with ASD. The student had come in without his homework, and the principal said (jokingly),

"It's okay, just a slap on the wrist," after which the young man began to panic. You probably know what the student thought. This is a good opportunity to remember that the language you use when talking with a person with ASD needs to often be concrete and specific. You don't need to talk like a robot, but you should avoid getting your point across with idioms and common expressions that may be misinterpreted. Be aware when you are having a conversation.

Your tone and pitch say a lot. There is no need to speak loudly to someone with ASD, nor is there a reason to speak in a baby voice or to speak too slowly. It is true you may have to speak with extra clarity, but not enough to sound like you are a computer-generated voice. Those with ASD hear you, but they may hear many things simultaneously. Thus, the clearer you speak, the better the chance of understanding.

Think about where you are having a conversation. Places that are loud and distracting may not be the best. Find a quiet spot or look to see if any distractions can be avoided. Many people with ASD prefer to have one-to-one conversations rather than group discussions, so think about the environment around you as you engage in conversation.

Bullying?

It is clear that bullying is something we shouldn't be doing, yet about 65 percent of students with ASD report that they are or have been bullied in their lives.[5] The worst time for bullying was reported to be from fifth through eighth grades. In a 2009 study, Susan Carter reported that the highest rates of bullying occurred with students who were previously diagnosed with Asperger's syndrome. She writes, "Children and adolescents with Asperger's syndrome have a myriad of challenges confronting them in the schools they attend. Many will never have the opportunity to express their talents because they are misunderstood, and often they are denied services because they are articulate, do well academically, and appear too bright. In actuality, many children with Asperger's syndrome have significant social deficits, severe sensory sensitivities, and are teased, isolated, and socially excluded by their peers."[6]

Dr. Connie Anderson, contributor for the Interactive Autism Network, reports that it is clear that bullying among the ASD community is much higher than in other groups, and often happens to trigger the meltdowns or aggressive outbursts. With Chicken Joe, discussed in chapter 1, kids were relentless in getting a response out of him for their own amusement. Dr. Anderson reports that the behavior and traits that were most associated with bullying an individual with ASD were clumsiness, poor hygiene, rigid rule keeping (enforcing rules when other children would not), continuing to talk about a favorite topic when others were bored or annoyed, frequent meltdowns, or general inflexibility.[7]

The fact that bullying is so common among the ASD community is alarming. It is crucial that not only adults but students as well begin to understand the ramifications of such behavior. If a child was suffering from anxiety, social withdrawal, depression, and lack of self-control, imagine what bullying does to these symptoms. Those with ASD may suffer any of these symptoms at a much higher rate due to bullying.

We can put in place any number of anti-bullying campaigns in a school or in a community; however, the most effective stance against bullying starts with you. Students with ASD can self-advocate but often need a voice to stand beside them. You must be the voice that they need. It is never okay to bully someone, but choosing a vulnerable victim who cannot retaliate is especially wrong.

What Can You Do about Bullying?

If you see something, say something. If you are not in a situation that may cause you physical harm, you may intervene. Friends or peers you know who engage in bullying need you to tell them to stop. In addition, you can explain why they should stop. You have read this book and know that hand flapping, for example, happens for a reason. Use your education to educate others who are ignorant of the topic.

When this won't work, you must tell school personnel. They need to be informed. You can do so anonymously. If you feel like you are ratting out a friend or another student, remember that usually the student being bullied is powerless to do anything. You need to stand up for what is right.

Be proactive. If you know someone who may become subject to bullying, offer your support and friendship. Help the student by modeling appropriate behavior and responses. Use your knowledge to educate others so that they develop a better understanding. Expand your circle of friends to include those who may be bullied otherwise.

Finally

There is a lot of information in this book that I hope will help you better understand the world of ASD. If there is one thing you take away, please remember that there are no hard and fast rules with ASD. Every individual is different and should be treated as such. The ASD community is as diverse as the non-ASD community and just as complex. Nothing that I have talked about applies to every person with ASD. The stories and experiences of those in this book are presented to give you insight into the population. You must take all this information and be able to adjust and modify it to fit your own unique experiences.

Perhaps the most important thing to ask yourself is whether your tolerance and understanding have grown, now that you understand something about ASD. The kids I went to school with who bullied those "standout" students would have been better informed today than they were back then. It is my hope that you are informed and can take an active step in providing a better community for those with special needs.

What is the biggest predictor for success for individuals with ASD? Probably you. We have a lot of work ahead to help integrate those with ASD into the general workings of society. Knowledge is the first step to helping all individuals with ASD have improved life experiences. Through acceptance of diversity, people can build a better community, one in which everyone has an equal playing field.

The Story of Jake

I met Jake when he was fourteen years old, a ninth grader in high school. I immediately recognized that he was a young man with a great many interesting gifts and talents. He was a prolific writer, had a wonderful imagination, was creative, had a voracious appetite for books, and had a memory for facts and subjects that went far beyond any ninth grader I knew. He was a young man with autism spectrum disorder and a young man with big dreams. He desired success in life, aspiring to be a filmmaker, and he wanted to find friends. He needed help organizing himself so that he could follow through on his plans. Often, his mind wandered in school and he spent half his time dreaming of stories and movies and half his time focused on school work.

Jake agreed to tell me his story for this chapter. Now at the age of twenty-five, he is a man who advocates for people with ASD. Through his lectures, films, and associations with advocacy groups, there is no one better to tell the story of ASD as it "happened to him."

As Jake tells his story, his words are filled with imagination and metaphors that he has found in books and movies. When I first began working with him, Jake almost always associated his own emotional state with that of a character from a book. I first had a difficult time understanding where Jake's world of internal characters ended and the world I knew began. For Jake, they were intertwined. It wasn't that he couldn't tell fantasy from reality; but Jake's emotions (fear, happiness, and especially love) were as passionate for a character in a book as they were for those closest to him in real life. In some ways, the books he read were more soothing and satisfying than the story of his own day-to-day adventures. Life was unscripted and could go anywhere. There was some safety in knowing the end of a story.

School wasn't always easy for him. He was subjected to teasing and bullying mostly because of his behavior. When Jake was having a hard time with his school work and controlling his anxiety, he was prone to outbursts and temper tantrums, which included banging his head on the desk and yelling. He quickly recognized his outbursts were not appropriate and was very remorseful in the aftermath.

In high school (in which I served as his counselor), he found new friends and teachers who helped him to manage his anxiety and his temper, and he did quite well for the years he attended. What was most interesting about Jake was his self-awareness and desire to become what he termed "a success." A success meant

Jake has become a successful young man. His journey there is a story worth telling! *Photo by Karen Waltuck*

having the behaviors of a typical high school student. It also meant becoming a world leader in helping others to be better people and not bully or tease others and, of course, becoming a storyteller through his scripts and films.

His ideas for becoming that success were big. He took many of his cues from historical Greek and Roman mythology, as well as popular movies. His journey in life was the story of one young man seeking to find an identity. But with such heroes as Odysseus and the gods on Mount Olympus, he had a lot of pressure to emulate those virtues. People generally do not live the life of a Greek god, nor can they defeat a cyclops, but Jake aspired to do so. For him, the cyclops was the bullies he would meet in life, and his job was to vanquish their powers.

While he associated his path in life with that of Frodo in *Lord of the Rings*, Jake's journey has been that of many typical teenagers (although Jake has had to work harder to achieve his success than most). The odds are against those with ASD for finding work, obtaining higher education, and living independently. Jake beat those odds and is a successful young adult. Jake was very aware of his ASD and now speaks proudly of how it has affected his life.

For Jake books were the first step in identifying his desires in life. He had a hard time relating to the outside world and instead turned inward to the pages of many stories. These books shaped his early life and his words. As you read his story, you will notice the many literary references he attaches to his own experiences.

His story begins:

> My name is Jacob. You may have heard stories about noble heroes going on quests to reach their goals, friends who would guide them on their journeys and the foes who would challenge them. And you've heard about the environments that would shape them in positive and negative ways. That is me! Most people with autism would have trouble fitting in at a very early age. Sure I did, I fit in, but it took a lot of hard work and energy and I wasn't always successful.
>
> Early on, a long, long time ago our story begins way back in 1991, when I was born. People didn't know I had autism. They didn't until I was diagnosed. I am not sure how old I was but when I grew from baby to child my adventures were about to begin. Amazing things were around every corner when I was a wee tyke. There were very kind people who took care of me, my teachers, family, and babysitters. It was fun being in school in kindergarten meeting amazing kids and participating in so many fun activities. The only problem was that I had a hard time paying attention. I was distracted by books and films. Films would pull me in and I was oblivious to the world outside. Books had the same effect on me. The first books I was ever exposed to were *The Very Hungry Caterpillar* and classic fairy tales and small fact books about animals and dinosaurs. There were also books on legendary creatures.

What did these books do for Jake? It was clear they were much more than good stories that he found interesting. Instead they became his world. It was as important a world as his daily life. Rather than experience life by interacting with other students or watching kids play and then joining in, Jake took his lessons for life from the pages of a book. Why were *The Very Hungry Caterpillar* and fairy tales so important to Jake?

> Stunning visuals by Eric Carle were mesmerizing, and sudden changes from a caterpillar to butterfly were the changes that I go through in my life. You start off "understanding yourself" like knowing what you are, and then you change your body but not what is inside you. The fairy tales amazed me because of the whimsy and darkness and they amazed me because of how you could use your skills to vanquish enemies, like I wanted to, meaning the bad kids who teased me, and fairy tale worlds can both terrify you and amaze you at the same time. I saw myself in them. Sometimes

> I felt connected to the characters, but I wondered to myself, "What part
> am I in this world? How would I be a part of this world?"

Despite most teachers encouraging their students to read, books often got in
the way of Jake's early education! He would be consumed with the stories and
the characters in books, and he often did not pay attention to the teacher. Jake
says it was the worst part of his early schooling. He would get a "time out" for
not paying attention. But he was keenly aware of his difficulties with paying attention. Sometimes he would force himself to try and pay attention, only to get
sidetracked by the running story in his mind.

> I felt like an outsider when my teachers thought I was not paying attention
> even though I was doing my best. What they didn't know was that my
> mind was structured in a way that made me different from other people.
> Images come in my mind and I could (and still can) see them. The images
> almost always block out other things. Sometimes I am not aware, some-
> times I am aware of them. They came by themselves without warning, but
> I enjoyed them very much.

It was clear that stories were a big part of Jake's life, but this did not mean
he did not want friends or did not want to interact with other kids in the outside
world. He tried but was not always successful.

> When I would interact with others I felt good, but it was (and sometimes
> still is) hard for me to get used to new things, so I might ignore them. I
> wanted friends (now I have a lot), but I always tried to use them as char-
> acters in a story and did not allow their own personality to shine! Like,
> for example, I cared deeply about women and girls my age; I had dreams
> of rescuing damsels in distress. I wanted to find a way of cultivating my
> dreams of finding women a safe paradise. I thought about turning these
> dreams into reality. I wanted to rescue these damsels, but later on I have
> come to realize girls should be free to make their own decisions. I would
> often act like a hero with a girl I liked rather than be myself. I would pre-
> tend I was recusing them from bullies or harm. In reality and film I have
> been exposed to very strong and "can do" women. Now I allow people to
> become who they want to be in my life and I have to let them be who they
> are. As an adult, I don't try and rescue women anymore.
>   I would play with other kids, but the books were drawing me in like
> a magnet. So I would mostly choose to read on my own. Even though I
> wanted to make friends, the pull of the books was too strong. I learned to
> read at a very young age at around 4 or 5. A lot of times we saw educa-

tional films based on the books I read, and I would be further pulled into the world of magical stories. I asked if I could take books and films home with me. I didn't bring them back because I wanted to show them to other people.

I enjoyed reading, science, and arts and crafts. In my grammar school the hardest part, again, was paying attention. I tried but I got overwhelmed and I did whatever I could to pay attention. I got carried away by many other things. In my mind I saw films and books and exciting things from what I read. It felt good to think about these things. It was cool to learn at school, but in my mind I wanted to escape and write stories, to share what I loved to the world. I listened carefully to the books my teachers read. The first novels I was exposed to were these classics: *The Lion, the Witch and the Wardrobe*, *The Secret Garden*, *Island of the Blue Dolphins*, *Charlotte's Web*, and *The Boxcar Children*. It was amazing to see live shows or movies based on these books with the class. I was mesmerized!

I would absorb a ton of information as easily as a sponge would absorb water. Sometimes I tuned things out, especially when people were trying to help me, but I knew that every person I came across was as caring as each lion in his pride, and as loving as the disciples of Moses. I know people were trying to help me, but I couldn't help it when I went into my own stories.

Jake's words remind us of the difficulty one with ASD has about taking perspective. Perhaps in his early years Jake saw other people as characters in his stories and not as individual beings with their own thoughts. The desire for relationships was there, but the empathy needed to interact was absent. He would inevitably rely on the scripts of books he read to process a relationship rather than have it unfold naturally. This may have been Jake's need for order and predictability as seen in many individuals with ASD. In any case, he worked hard at trying to understand the complexities of relationships.

Jake also had a tough time understanding and explaining his own emotions. He often related his moods to characters he read in books or saw in films. For example, when he was upset he would reply that he felt like "the character in *Toy Story* who cannot find his way home." Always on point with his descriptions, Jake would explain himself through imaginary characters, not attaching the emotion to his own experience or state of mind.

A lot of time as a child I was happy, and sometimes I got overwhelmed when I got into trouble. I did sometimes tantrum, but mostly cried. When the teachers had harsh and stern voices it made me scared because it would be unexpected. It would be like if you were a mouse and you didn't know the snake was behind you when it struck. I'd get overwhelmed by things that were way too hard or intense for me. My stomach would twist and my heart would beat faster and my mind would be crowded like cars in the road (traffic jam). These feelings still happen today, but a lot of times I have better coping mechanisms. I was the cowardly lion in the *Wizard of Oz*; I had to find my courage!

It seems that Jake also had the classic sensory issues that may accompany ASD. Teachers' loud voices would startle him and create either a tantrum or crying fit. The physical symptoms that come from the overwhelming stimulus of his environment were at times too much.

Sometimes loud noises; when I hear a loud noise bad thoughts fill my head. They make me think of people getting hurt; a loud noise would create terrible scenes in my mind of people getting killed, and fighting and slaughtering. I was afraid of being startled by loud noises or teachers' voices when I was young. Sometimes the rough earth, like the feel of the ground, would make me upset. It would feel harsh and terrible and I would cry because it felt painful to touch the ground. So, loud noises, the things I touched, and a series of temptations and distractions make school hard and challenging at first. I always thought to myself, "Should I react in a bad way or keep myself calm?" Sometimes I could keep calm but I needed help.

He also had difficulty with letting go of the past. Things that happened months or even years prior would still haunt his mind, and often create extra stress and anxiety.

I get super-overwhelmed by situations and events that have happened in the past and they stay in my mind. Like when my grandfather passed away or when I lost people I loved, or when I thought about how the world is not suitable for people with high functioning autism (and I am not just talking about myself). At camp, many people bullied me or expressed no sympathy. I do whatever I can to let the past experiences go, to make my world a better place, but it gets stuck for a while (it is like seeing film characters succeed and fail). Years can go by but some things feel like they happened yesterday.

But Jake did not have to go it alone in his early years. He was fortunate to have a strong family and series of caregivers who helped him develop his sense of control and regulate his behavior. While people around him provided much of the support, he most often found support in the films, books, and stories he watched and read.

Lots of people helped me; they cheered me up when I got sad. Even on my bad days they helped me in an uncomfortable environment. It was a good thing I steered clear of stereotypes. For example, many brothers and sisters constantly fight. But my big sister was nurturing and compassionate and strong willed. She took great care of me. Most people would be nervous about going to the doctor or dentist, but my pediatrician and my dentist were gentle and their offices were comforting. They knew I would be uncomfortable and act harshly to their probing and prodding, but they were very kind to me. Another thing that helped me keep calm was the many films I saw. The first ones I was exposed to were short films and especially classic Disney films, especially the big four that started the nineties renaissance and opened the door to Disney's modern age. I was also exposed to live action films like *Fly Away Home*.

These films, the animation and stories, pulled me in, each focusing on a hero going after his goals. Like me. But I knew by watching them over and over, whether or not the characters would be successful. The stories made me laugh, smile, shiver, and cry at the same time. I felt like the characters in the films. I felt I was opening myself to the world, just as each character does in unpredictable ways, but safely. Of all the years that shaped my childhood 1998 was the possibly absolute best. It all comes down to these three reasons.

First, because of the great amount of amazing animated films released that year. Audiences were enthralled by Nickelodeon's famous talking babies, a west African youth with a heart of a lion, an inventive ant going against overwhelming odds saving his colony (one of Warner Brothers' most underrated gems). DreamWorks took the exodus to a whole new level, and many an audiences' first cinematic exposure to a feminist heroine alongside hilarious dragons, and, pardon my French, "badass" villains.

The second reason 1998 was an important year in shaping my life was that this was a year I met many friends I would remember for years to come. My babysitters Jennifer and John took care of me when mom and dad were away. My pets, Felix the cat, Oscar the tortoise, and Sally and Lisa the red-eared slider turtles were there to keep me company. And along came Max. A part beagle, part border collie dog John gave to me. Because he felt this dog would be pretty good around children. Initially he was named Jake. But when the pooch set paw on the family soil he was dubbed Max. To be exact the people who came along in my life for the first time were my school friends. A sweet Japanese American girl, Yumi, would become one of my crushes. Henry, Sam, and Rustle, and Justin were among others I learned how to appreciate. This was the first time I had pretty close friends. It was a thrill meeting new friends, these friends became pretty close.

Third greatest thing of 1998 was the music! Every time I turned on my home radio channel on "special celebrations" I was exposed to a series of songs by wonderful musicians, the Beatles, Magical David, who I heard when I was much younger. Country singer Tom Chapin, Tracy Chapman, and Enya who, I kid you not, my mom listened to when I was in her womb. So simply put 1998 was one of those rare years that started and ended with a major bang.

We see what made this year and the years surrounding so important. Jake's memories focus on films first, friends second, and music third. It is so easy to see the essential element of Jake's emotional being as the story line in a movie. He makes the comment that he knew in advance what outcome the characters would have. This was a great comfort to him as his own life, the day-to-day situations, were not scripted and could not be predicted. But would this always be an important factor in Jake's life? Would he begin to live outside of his scripts and stories? Jake continues,

When 2000 rolled around, a new millennium began not just for me but for everyone. People were eager to start a new life and shape their lives in beautiful ways. I was eager to see new things around every corner, meet a lot of wonderful new friends. It seemed like it would be an optimistic time for me, more events to fuel my dreams. Unfortunately, when the world changed so did I. In a lot of great stories the hero is introduced with passion, someone or something he loves and has a flaw. It seems as though our hero or heroine is about to have a fresh start, but then baboom! Their world is turned upside down and insult is added to injury. This is exactly what happened to me. When the September 11th attacks rolled around I had to be pulled out of grammar school. I was forced into a very, very grown-up world. It was a lot of pressure to place on a ten-year-old like myself. Without that event, I would have had a much brighter childhood like I did in my early years.

Jake is the hero. His life is turned upside down. As you will see, during these years of the changing millennium, he was the hero he so vividly describes in his favorite stories. While he talks about the events of 9/11 causing great harm to him emotionally, other factors would influence his state of being. He continues,

In a new camp it seemed I would make a lot of friends like I did in my previous camp. Sure there were some good friends to remember but many of them bullied me for my love of Disney films and treated me in ways that would overwhelm me. There were also kids acting like rude adults. There had to be reasons behind these behaviors. One reason maybe was the films they were exposed to. Another reason was they were scarred by 9/11 or maybe it was jealousy or prejudice. There are many things that can put a hero in a rough state or make a villain bad. Heroes can be put in rough states because they are caught up in something that turns their world upside down, or maybe they struggle with a change, or maybe they are in a world where few people understand what they are going though or appreciate their goals. A villain can turn bad because of how their world shapes them, or they can be under someone's shadow. Or they take things in the wrong direction like *Toy Story 3*'s Lotso. Or they might be driven by greed, revenge, or an appetite in self-indulgence. This makes them the exact opposite and a genuine threat to the main character.

After 9/11 and the bullying, my autism took my life to a whole new level and the anxiety gauge went up. My mind was crowded with a lot of very bad thoughts, even though I tried to seek the good in the world. (Admittedly, there were a lot of amazing events to remember like going to Walt Disney World with my grandparents, being in shows and dances at camp, and seeing so many fun movies.) Being overwhelmed by 9/11 and the bullying the pressure drove me to do things that were not very good.

Now these things ranged from throwing tantrums, crying, picking fights, having scuffles, and going on not so good websites (with monsters and violence). I wanted to revive those things that happened to me in the past. I looked at these violent things because they made me think about the bad stuff that happened. I can't explain why, but I thought if I understood the evil, it would make me feel better. I also tried to relive the good things by looking at old movies and books I loved, but what I ended up looking up was bad. Those websites involved females getting captured by bad guys and monstrous creatures. As I said in the beginning I wanted to escape from the pressure, but what I did only boosted it up. I wanted to quell the pressure. I wanted to fight all the obstacles in my path, fight the villains (metaphorically) and meet foes to face. I thought by looking at the evil I would understand its power. When I conquered those foes I would have become the greatest, a very special person, feel good and be good to my family. Unfortunately, doing these things didn't work, and often got me into trouble.

As for the films I saw there were a few good ones I remember from those times like the wonders of Pixar, and *The Lion, the Witch and the*

Wardrobe, *Peter Pan* 2003, and many others. But a lot of the films I saw had little to offer compared to the films that shaped my childhood in the past. Whether it was the not so good storytelling, or the films revolving around characters that had no empathy or ability to overcome their flaws and often doing stupid things, I am not sure. In other words I found out even after those tough times in the thousands, I found out that for every wonder there was a blunder. Later on it was easy to see how many films won Oscars or Razzies. (That was a metaphor for my behaviors.)

Actions can change the course of history. Actions can get people to look up to you. My mind was mixing stories with each other. That is to say, my life stories with those others had written. I realized I could combine the two and use my life to create the perfect story, one that would have lifted my spirit to new heights. I made short films with a friend Joe when I was twelve. The films were about a cat fighting a hunter, a film based on a children's book about bathtub toys in the ocean and toys on a wild goose chase. Filmmaking gave me the courage to give ideas to others and create a world that would be comfortable for me. I wanted to share them so others understood me. By creating my own film I created my own world, like in books and stories. I could push away bad memories and make room for the positive.

After two middle schools (both had their ups and downs), I started high school at a new academy. It would open my doors to a bright new future. By introducing me to a series of amazing new friends and teachers, I wouldn't play around the high school stereotype failures. I have to admit the work was overwhelming, but there were some great times. Along with so many fun experiences, like I was excited to visit Ellis Island to look at my ancestry. I felt close to my grandfather on that trip. Autism at this new school was well known, and brought these people cared about people with disabilities, so the environment was calm, medium ambiance, and the teachers were mostly very kind and brought lots of fun books to read. They didn't give me too much homework, the lessons were many times easy to understand and I developed career opportunities, like an internship at the Museum of Natural History (one of my favorite places in the city as a tour guide in the dinosaur exhibit). In those years there were so many fun trips with my family, like swimming in the Bayo Bay and with dolphins in Cuba. It seemed as though high school (the environment I was in) gave me courage.

But then came one of the hardest years I went through in 2008. Not only was this one of the two years when an economic recession was looming over the city and taking away jobs, like the Kraken taking sailors from the ships, but the first half of the summer was the worst bullying experience I ever encountered. When I went to Belize with a summer camp, it seemed it would give me a great opportunity to experience a brave new world. The environment was friendly but almost all of the campers and counselors were not. They teased me, I tried to stop the bullies but the teasing pushed me into the ground like an old stick. They teased me about violence and made jokes about murder, rape, and called my father a murderer. The counselors did nothing to stop it and left me alone with the bullies. I tried to reason with them and tried to fight them, but I felt like Odysseus and his men shut away in the cave of the dreaded cyclops, Polyphemus. I also felt like a dolphin calf separated from his mother in a very large sea. After two weeks of trouble (even though there were a few good times like swimming in cool water and exploring marketplaces and caves), I went home and explained to my mother what had happened. The bullies put me down but never broke my spirit. My mom was angry at the counselors for not doing anything about this; it was a very good thing that she stood up for me. But the bullying took many months to overcome.

Riding on a cruise ship during a family vacation (I tried to put the bullying aside), I had so much fun with my family and sister riding around the sea. With a lot of intense things on my mind, I was unaware of how successful films from the likes of J. J. Abrams and David Fincher were doing in the theaters because of the bullying. (Years later I took the time to understand the success of those films.)

Even though there were many blunders (like the movie *Land of the Lost*), there were other things that were wonderful. A year later, five redeeming moments came to my life. One of them was when I worked with film tutors Josh and Justin on two short films. One was about a teenage boy who defends his girlfriend from bullies. This helped me to overcome the bullying that was inflicted upon me (and we made a film set in an environment like Belize). The other film was about a young man who bargains with a fairy to please his girlfriend.

The second important event was when I starred in a play that would lead me to pursue my dream of being in show business and making incredible movies. That play was *The Wizard of Oz* where I played the helpful and eccentric scarecrow. I was with a brilliant cast including good friends. Those performances made my heart swell like a balloon. They helped me overcome the stress of an impending graduation.

The third redeeming moment was graduating high school. It was such a thrill. Especially having so many friends and relatives to support me on the way. I would be on top of the world. I made it and I had become a great student. I passed all necessary state tests to achieve my goal. But I was nervous. What was next? Where would I be in the next few years?

The fourth special moment of 2009 is when I went with my dear friend Kristal to the bustling mountains of Machu Picchu, in Peru. There, I went on an inspiring adventure tending to orphaned children, and leading an adventurous team to the top of a mountain in Machu Picchu, I overcame my fear of heights. On the way I was sweating and tired, but my heart was telling me to never give up.

The fifth great moment or I should say moments, were the great number of movies that came out that year, live action and animated. James Cameron took filmmaking to new heights with *Avatar*. There were also delightful animated times like *Coraline*, *Fantastic Mr. Fox*, *Up*, *The Princess and the Frog*, and *The Secret of Kels*. Going to the premier of *The Princess and the Frog* with Justin was a real treat. After Disney had a series of struggles and flops, I was hoping Disney would bring its studio back on its feet and carry on its legacy with its stunning hand-drawn animation, colorful characters, and powerful storytelling. Going to the premier and learning to draw from a Disney animator Anthony Derosa who I met at the premier inspired me to want to work with Disney. Sure *Princess and the Frog* brought back hand-drawn animation and was inspiring, but it was easy to see, one would say, why Pixar was in power at that time.

But the fun didn't last long. That same year when the economic recession swamped the United States, my dad's treasured restaurant was taken away from him, putting the entire family into a wreck. My anxiety gauge went up once again. From 2010 to 2013, the family scrimped and saved and struggled, I still struggled with my feelings but enrolled in college prep at a program affiliated with my high school. This program where (I kid you not) they didn't give the people any homework.

At the end of 2013, another chapter in my life opened up. I was able to rekindle my ability to experience magical environments when I went to Hershey's Chocolate World in Pennsylvania. Around that time Disney brought its studio back on its feet with a new hit that like a few films before it opened the chapter to a revival. That film was *Frozen*. Seeing how well Disney did was a metaphor that there was a chance to improve upon my ability to cope with certain situations and be more aware of other people. In 2014, came a situation which was exciting and overwhelming at the same time. The good news was that after four to five years of struggling, my dad opened up a new restaurant. I started college that year at a community college in New York where I aced my first class, Fundamentals of Speech.

When I was told it was time for my family to move out of our home, I became so overwhelmed that I threw a fit. I was scared and angry about leaving my old home and special things from the past. When I moved I took my time to calm down, it took weeks and months to get over the stress.

College was overwhelming and still is, but I do whatever I can to deal with the stress. Now as a young man I am learning to cope with stress and anxiety by counting down from ten, taking deep breaths and being more aware of my body and tension. I also meditate and find time to relax. I will admit some things still throw me into a fit, but I am much better able to calm myself down.

The biggest challenge for me today is finding opportunities and for building my future and a future for all "aspies."[1] I want to balance the past with the present and the future, take the time to move on, and conquer my fears of missing out on opportunities and falling into the stereotype fit that people have of ASD. Another hope I have is to go around the world and advocate for people with autism and help others learn from the mistakes they made in the past. I am trying to make something better. When I was volunteering for ASD friendly spaces theater for *The Lion King* on Broadway I heard about a kid who was watching the play *The King and I* who had a crying fit when he saw the intense whipping scene. The crowd accused the mother of bringing the child to the play negligently and blamed the child for disrupting the play. Both were, how do I say it, "booted out." This is not fair and needs an advocate like me to solve these types of problems.

There are many delightful films, plays, books that took me into their world. Support from friends and family that have been helping me overcome those stressful times, one day at a time. My experiences, people I cared about, and the lessons I have learned inspired me to write many stories such as the Island of Peace, Modern Myths, Big Taste in the Big Easy, Kingdom of the Fairies, Curse of the Vampire, the Savanah, and more.

I had many jobs during my time as a young adult like at the Maysles Film Institute. I also worked at the Tribeca Film Festival and now am proud to say I work at Ecclectic Encore Warehouse. There I organize props rented for stage plays and films. It is amazing work to hold the important props used on stage and screen.

But Jake has even more to be proud of. During the summer he attended the Zeno Mountain Farm, which was very different from the Belize camp. This was a program for young adults with special needs and offered a filmmaking program. Not only did Jake participate in several films, he was an important character.

Every person was welcome, even those with autism and other disabilities because that's what the camp is all about. I starred in two films from Zeno

Mountain Farm, *Finding Zac Efron* and *Bulletproof*, a wild west film. There is a documentary about Zeno farm called *Becoming Bulletproof*. Being in a film inspires me to work in the film business and present things to others in a good way.

The documentary *Becoming Bulletproof* was released in 2015 and has received critical acclaim. Some critics suggested it be nominated for an Oscar.[2] However, it was not.

My journey has gone from wondrous beginnings, to tumultuous adolescence all the way to an adulthood that has given me hope. Some events inspire me so much that I want to do them again and channel them into positive opportunities for other people. I feel if I don't do this as soon as possible and advocate for other people, the dreams of other people with ASD will fade away like the setting sun and wither like an old tree. I also hope that I will always have extra support from my mentors, family, and special friends to improve my behaviors and get to develop an understanding of how well I am doing.

Jake's passion to educate the world about ASD led him to the United Nations World Autism Conference, where he was a featured speaker. *Photo by Karen Waltuck*

The world is full of people who aspire to achieve their goals. It does not mean they have to become president or someone famous. It only means that they have an opportunity to pursue their interests and make a life that suits their needs. Jake has done this. He has had to work harder than most to get where he is today as a college student and someone who is active in the world of film. We can be inspired by Jake's ability to deal with pressures that the average person does not deal with and still come out on top!

Notes

Foreword

1. Benjamin Zablotsky, Lindsey I. Black, Matthew J. Maenner, Laura A. Schieve, and Stephen J. Blumberg, "Estimated Prevalence of Autism and Other Developmental Disabilities Following Questionnaire Changes in the 2014 National Health Interview Survey," *National Health Statistics Reports*, no. 87, November 13, 2015.

a. Carol Blessing, Barbara Levits, and Mitchell Levitz, *Policy and Practice Brief: Establishing a New Standard for Inclusion in the Classroom*, Ithaca, NY: Cornell University Press, 2003, digitalcommons.ilr.cornell.edu/cgi/viewcontent.cgi?article=1106&context=edicollect.

Chapter 1

a. Ryan Jaslow, "Survey Finds 63% of Students with Autism Bullied," *CBS News*, March 13, 2012, www.cbsnews.com/news/survey-finds-63-of-children-with-autism-bullied/.
b. American Psychiatric Association, *Diagnostic and Statistical Manual of Mental Disorders, 5th ed. (DSM-5)*, Washington, DC: American Psychiatric Association, 2013.

Chapter 2

1. Centers for Disease Control, "Data and Statistics," www.cdc.gov/ncbddd/autism/data.html (accessed June 22, 2015).
2. Nicole Ostrow, "Autism Costs More Than 2 Million Dollars over Patient's Life," *Bloomberg Business*, June 9, 2014, www.bloomberg.com/news/articles/2014-06-09/autism-costs-more -than-2-million-over-patient-s-life.
3. Center for Disease Control, "Data and Statistics."
4. American Psychiatric Association, *Diagnostic and Statistical Manual of Mental Disorders*, 5th ed. (*DSM-5*), Washington, DC: American Psychological Association, 2013.
5. Johnny Matson and Marie Nebel-Schwalm, "Comorbid Psychopathology with Autism Spectrum Disorder in Children: An Overview, *Research in Developmental Disabilities* 28 (2007): 341–352.
6. Gagan Joshi, Carter Petty, Janet Wozniak, Aude Henin, Ronna Fried, Maribel Gald, Meghan Kotarski, Sarah Walls, and Joseph Biederman, "The Heavy Burden of Psychiatric Comorbidity in Youth with Autism Spectrum Disorders: A Large Comparative Study of a Psychiatrically Referred Population," *Journal of Autism and Developmental Disorders* 40, no. 11 (November 2010): 1361–1370.
7. American Psychiatric Association, *DSM-5*.

8. Karen Rowan, "Why Kids with Autism May Avoid Eye Contact," *Live Science*, June 5, 2013, livescience.com/37167-autism-avoid-eye-contact-brain.html.

9. Adam Zaidel, Robin Goin-Kochel, and Dora Angelaki, "Self-Motion Perception in Autism Is Compromised by Visual Noise but Integrated Optimally across Multiple Senses," *Proceedings of the National Academy of Sciences* 10, no. 12 (2015): 6461–6466.

10 Christine B., "Sensory Integration Therapy for Autism," LovetoKnow, autism.lovetoknow .com/Sensory_Integration_Therapy_for_Autism.

11. William Heward, *Exceptional Children: An Introduction to Special Education*, New York: Pearson Education, 2006, pp. 268–271.

---

a. Philip Reyes, "Eye Contact," *Faith, Hope, and Love . . . with Autism* (blog), January 24, 2015, faithhopeloveautism.blogspot.com/2015/01/eye-contact.html. Reprinted with permission from Lisa Reyes.

b. Kay Sikich, "Early Childhood Educator," Community Education, www.district196.org/ec/Teacherprofiles/KaySikich.cfm.

c. Leslie Packer, "Overview of Tourette's Syndrome," Tourette Syndrome "Plus," last updated March 2015, www.tourettesyndrome.net/disorders/tourette%E2%80%99s-syndrome/overview-of-tourettes-syndrome/.

d. Rachel Coulter, "Understanding the Visual Symptoms of Individuals with Autism Spectrum Disorder," *Optometry and Vision* 40, no. 3 (2009): 164–175.

e. David Evans, Kristin Canavera, F. Lee Kleinpeter, Elise Maccubbin, and Ken Taga, "The Fears, Phobia, and Anxieties of Children with Autism Spectrum Disorders and Down Syndrome: Comparisons with Developmentally and Chronologically Age Matched Children," *Child Psychiatry Human Development* 36, no. 1 (September 2005): 3–26.

Chapter 3

1. Leo Kanner, "Autistic Disturbances of Affective Contact," *Nervous Child* 2 (1943): 217–250.

2. Hans Asperger, "Autistic Psychopaths in Childhood," in *Autism and Asperger Syndrome*, ed. Uta Frith, New York: Cambridge University Press, 1991, pp. 37–92.

3. L. Coates, "History of Asperger Syndrome," Asperger Syndrome.Me.UK: Offering Help and Support, www.asperger-syndrome.me.uk/history.html.

4. Lorna Wing, "Asperger Syndrome: A Clinical Account," *Psychological Medicine* 11 (1981): 115–129.

5. John Watson, *Behaviorism*, New York: People's Institute Publishing Company, 1924, p. 104.

6. Bruno Bettelheim, *The Empty Fortress*, New York: Free Age Press, 1967.

7. Temple Grandin, *The Autistic Brain*, New York: Mariner Books, 2014.

8. National Consumer League Statistic, "Survey: One Third of American Parents Mistakenly Link Vaccines to Autism" (press release), National Consumers League, April 2, 2014, www .nclnet.org/survey_one_third_of_american_parents_mistakenly_link_vaccines_to_autism.

9. A. Wakefield, S. Murch, A. Anthony, J. Linnell, D. Carson, M. Malik, M. Berelowitz, A. Dhillon, M. Thompson, P. Harvey, A. Valentine, S. Davies, and J. Walker-Smith, "Ileallymphoind-Nodular Hyperplasia, Non-specific Colitis, and Pervasive Developmental Disorder in Children," *Lancet* 351 (1998): 637–641.

10. Gardiner Harris, "Journal Retracts 1998 Paper Linking Autism to Vaccines," *New York Times*, February 2, 2010.

11. Therese Gronborg, Diana Schendel, and Erik Parner, "Recurrence of Autism Spectrum Disorders in Full- and Half-Siblings and Trends over Time: A Population-Based Cohort Study," *Journal of the American Medical Association: Pediatrics* 167, no. 10 (2013): 947–953.

a. Ahbishek Ashok, John Baugh, and Vikram Yeragani, "Paul Eugen Bleuler and the Origin of the Term Schizophrenia (Schizopreniegruppe)," *Indian Journal of Psychiatry* 54, no. 1 (2012): 95–96.

b. Leo Kanner, "Autistic Disturbances of Affective Contact," *Nervous Child* 2 (1943): 217–250.

c. John Donovan and Caren Zucker, "Autism's First Child," *Atlantic* 10 (2010), www.theatlantic.com/magazine/archive/2010/10/autisms-first-child/308227/.

d. Hans Asperger, "Autistic Psychopaths in Childhood," in *Autism and Asperger Syndrome*, ed. Uta Frith, New York: Cambridge University Press, 1991, pp. 37–92.

e. U.S. Department of Health & Human Services, "IRBs and Assurances," HHS.gov, www.hhs.gov/ohrp/assurances/index.html#.

f. Bruno Bettelheim, *The Uses of Enchantment*, New York: Alfred A. Knopf, 1976.

g. Maria Davis, interview with author, September 1, 2015.

Chapter 4

1. Shlomi Haar, Sigal Berman, Marlene Behrmann, and Ilan Dinstein, "Anatomical Abnormalities in Autism?" *Cereb Cortex* 242 (October 2014), cercor.oxfordjournals.org/content/early/2014/10/14/cercor.bhu242.abstract.

2. Nicholas Lange, Brittany Travers, Erin Bigler, Molly Prigge, Alyson Froehlich, Jared Nielsen, Annahir Cariello, Brandon Zielinski, Jeffrey Anderson, P. Thomas Fletcher, Andrew Alexander, and Janet Lainhart, "Longitudinal Volumetric Brain Changes in Autism Spectrum Disorder Ages 6–35," *Autism Research* 8, no. 1 (February 2015): 82–93.

3. Christopher Gregg, "Decoding Autism," *Science Translational Medicine* 5, no. 216 (2013): 208–216.

4. John Swann and Solomon Moshe, "On the Basic Mechanisms of Infantile Spasm," in *Jasper's Basic Mechanisms of the Epilepsies*, 4th ed., ed. Jeffery Noebles and Michael Rogawski, Internet version, 2013, pp. 272–283.

5. Aarti Nair, Jeffrey Treiber, Dinesh K. Shukla, Patricia Shih, and Ralph-Axel Muller, "Impaired Thalamocortical Connectivity in Autism Spectrum Disorder: A Study of Functional and Anatomical Connectivity," *Brain* 139, no. 2 (June 2013): 1942–1955.

6. Jose Maximo, Elyse Cadena, and Rajesh Kana, "The Implications of Brain Connectivity in the Neuropsychology of Autism," *Neuropsychology Review* 24, no. 1 (March 2014): 16–31.

7. Christopher Keown, Patricia Shih, Aarti Nair, Nick Peterson, Mark Mulvey, and Ralph-Axel Muller, "Local Functional Overconnectivity in Posterior Brain Regions Is Associated with Symptom Severity in Autism Spectrum Disorder," *Cell Reports* 5, no. 3 (November 2013): 567–572.

8. Paul Wang, "Does Brain Activity Interfere with Sociability?" Autism Speaks, February 3, 2012, www.autismspeaks.org/science/science-news/autismbusy-brains-does-brain-activity-interfere-sociability,.

9. Amanda Kahn, Aarti Nair, Christopher Keow, Michael Datko, Alan Lincoln, and Ralph-Axel Muller, "Cerebro-Cerebellar Resting State Functional Connectivity in Children and

Adolescents with Autism Spectrum Disorder," *Biological Psychiatry*, March 31, 2015, www .sciencedirect.com/science/article/pii/S0006322315002735.

10. Emily Anthes, "Autism Brains Are Overly Connected, Studies Find," Spectrum, December 2013, sfari.org/news-and-opinion/news/2013/autism-brains-are-overly-connected-studies -find.

11. Darold Treffert, "The Savant Syndrome: An Extraordinary Condition. A Synopsis: Past, Present, Future," *Philosophical Transactions* 364, no. 1522 (May 2009): 1351–1357.

12. J. Landon Down, MD, "Observations on an Ethnic Classification of Idiots," *London Hospital Reports* 3 (1866): 259–262.

13. Temple Grandin, *The Autistic Brain*, New York: Mariner Books, 2014.

14. Joseph Call and Michael Tomasello, "A Nonverbal False Belief Task: The Performance of Children and Great Apes," *Child Development* 70, no. 2 (March/April 1999): 381–395.

15. Johanna Lantz, "Theory of Mind in Autism: Development, Implications, and Interventions," Indiana Resource Center for Autism, University of Indiana, dev.iidc.indiana.edu/pages/ Theory-of-Mind-in-Autism-Development-Implications-and-Intervention; Patricia Howlin, Simon Baron-Cohen, and Julie Hadwin, *Teaching Children with Autism to Mind-Read: A Practical Guide for Teachers and Parents*, West Sussex, England: Wiley, 1998.

a. Suzana Herculano-Houzel, "The Human Brain in Numbers: A Linearly Scaled-Up Primate Brain," *Frontiers in Human Neuroscience*, November 2009, journal.frontiersin.org/article/ 10.3389/neuro.09.031.2009/full.

Chapter 5

1. Miriam Liss, Celine Saulnier, Deborah Fein, and Marcel Kinsbourne, "Sensory and Attention Abnormalities in Autistic Spectrum Disorders," *Autism* 10, no. 2 (2006): 155–180.

2. Centers for Disease Control, "Signs and Symptoms," www.cdc.gov/ncbddd/autism/signs .html.

3. Temple Grandin, *The Autistic Brain*, Boston: Houghton Mifflin, 2013.

4. Donna Williams, *Nobody Nowhere: The Remarkable Autobiography of an Autistic Girl*, New York: Times Books, 1992, p. 37.

5. Sandra Tosta, "The Autistic Child: More Than Meets the Eye," *BrainBlogger* (blog), March 2, 2013, brainblogger.com/2013/03/02/the-autistic-child-more-than-meets-the-eye/.

6. Lindsey Biel and Nancy Peske, *Raising a Sensory Smart Child: The Definitive Handbook for Helping Your Child with Sensory Processing Issues*, New York: Penguin Books, 2009.

a. Naoki Higashida, *The Reason I Jump: The Inner Voice of a Thirteen-Year-Old Boy with Autism*, New York: Random House, 2013, p. 51.

b. Arthur Fleischmann and Carly Fleischmann, *Carly's Voice: Breaking through Autism*, New York: Touchstone, 2012, p. 376.

c. Carly Fleischmann, "FAQ," Carly's Voice: Changing the World. of Autism, carlysvoice.com/ home/faq/.

d. Erin Polk, "Adult with Nonverbal Autism Shares What Sensory Overload Feels Like for Her," *The Mighty*, January 20, 2015, themighty.com/2015/01/adult-with-nonverbal-autism-shares -what-sensory-overload-feels-like-for-her/.

e. Lindsey Biel and Nancy Peske, *Raising a Sensory Smart Child: The Definitive Handbook for Helping Your Child with Sensory Processing Issues*, New York: Penguin Books, 2009.
f. Biel and Peske, *Raising a Sensory Smart Child*.

Chapter 6

1. U.S. Department of Education, National Center for Education Statistics, *Digest of Education Statistics, 2013* (NCES 2015–011), Table 204.60, nces.ed.gov/fastfacts/display.asp?id=59.
2. Louis Hagopian, Samantha Hardesty, and Meagan Gregory, "Overview and Summary of Scientific Support for Applied Behavior Analysis," KennedyKrieger.org, www.kennedykrieger .org/sites/kki2.com/files/aba-scientific-support-revised-7-2015.pdf.
3. Ruth Campbell, "The Processing of Audio-Visual Speech: Empirical and Neural Base," *Philosophical Transactions, the Royal Society of London*, September 7, 2007, www.ncbi.nlm .nih.gov/pmc/articles/PMC2606792/.
4. Lori Frost and Andrew Boundy, *PECS: The Picture Exchange Communication System*, 2nd ed., Newark, DE: Pyramid Educational Consultants, 2002.
5. National Institute of Child Health and Human Development, "Medication Treatment," last reviewed November 30, 2012, www.nichd.nih.gov/health/topics/autism/conditioninfo/Pages/ medication-treatment.aspx.
6. Roman Tyzio, "Oxytocin-Mediated GABA Inhibition during Delivery Attenuates Autism Pathogenesis in Rodent Offspring," *Science* 343, no. 6171 (February 2014): 675–679.

a. Noah C., interview with author, October 24, 2015.
b. Authur Fleischmann and Carly Fleischmann, *Carly's Voice: Breaking through Autism*, New York: Touchstone, 2012, p.118.
c. Noah, interview.
d. Stanley Greenspan, Serena Wieder, and Robin Simons, *The Child with Special Needs*, New York: Perseus Books, 1998.

Chapter 7

1. Food and Agricultural, "Chapter 2: Organization of the United Nations, Effects of Stress and Injury on Meat By-Product Quality," FAO Corporate Document Repository, www.fao.org/ docrep/003/x6909e/x6909e04.htm.
2. Temple Grandin, *The Autistic Brain: Helping Different Kinds of Minds Succeed*, Boston: Houghton Mifflin Harcourt, 2013, p. 3.
3. Sy Montgomery, *Temple Grandin: How the Girl Who Loved Cows Embraced Autism and Changed the World*, New York: Houghton Mifflin Books for Children, 2012, pp. 6–8.
4. Montgomery, *Temple Grandin*, p. 104.
5. Alexander Yee and Kondo Shigeru, "5 Trillion Digits of Pi—New World Record," Number World, August 2, 2010, www.numberworld.org/misc_runs/pi-5t/announce_en.html.
6. Daniel Tammet, *Born on a Blue Day*, New York: Free Press/Simon and Schuster, 2007, pp. 22–26.
7. Tammet, *Born on a Blue Day*, pp. 77–78.

8. Simon Baron-Cohen, Daniel Bor, Jac Billington, Sally Wheelwright, and Chris Ashwin, "Savant Memory in a Man with Colour Form-Number Synaesthesia and Asperger Syndrome," *Journal of Consciousness Studies* 14, nos. 9–10 (2007): 243–245.

9. "Kim Peek, Medicine Obituaries," *Telegraph*, October 10, 2010, www.telegraph.co.uk/news/obituaries/medicine-obituaries/6867567/Kim-Peek.html.

10. Fran Peek, *The Real Rain Man: Kim Peek*, California: Harkness Publishing, 1997.

a. Temple Grandin, "Calming Effects of Deep Touch Pressure in Patients with Autistic Disorder, College Students, and Animals," *Journal of Child and Adolescent Psychopharmacology* 2, no. 1 (1992), 155.

b. Temple Grandin, "Keys to Successful Living, Employment and a Good Social Life for Individuals with Autism and Asperger's," Autism Research Institute, www.autism.com/grandin_independence.

c. Grandin, "Keys to Successful Living."

d. Daniel Tammet, *Born on a Blue Day*, London: Hodder Paperbacks, 2007, pp. 2–3.

e. Tammet, *Born on a Blue Day*, pp. 178–179.

f. Fran Peek, *The Real Rain Man: Kim Peek*, California: Harkness Publishing, 1997, pp. iii–vi.

g. Ed Pilkington, "The Real Rain Man Dies of a Heart Attack in Hometown of Salt Lake City," *Guardian*, November 2009.

h. Jenny Johnston, "The Truth about My Asperger's: Susan Boyle Reveals Just How Difficult It Is Living with a Condition That Makes Her Behaviour So Very Unpredictable," *DailyMail.com*, November 14, 2014, www.dailymail.co.uk/femail/article-2828626/The-truth-Asperger-s-Susan-Boyle-reveals-just-difficult-living-condition-makes-behaviour-unpredictable.html#ixzz3mIL35FwX.

Chapter 8

1. Naomi Davis and Alice Carter, "Parenting Stress in Mothers and Fathers of Toddlers with Autism Spectrum Disorders: Associations with Child Characteristics," *Journal of Autism and Developmental Disorders* 38, no. 7 (August 2008): 1278–1291.

2. Ewa Pisula, "Parenting Stress in Mothers and Fathers of Children with Autism Spectrum Disorders," chapter 5 in *A Comprehensive Book on Autism Spectrum Disorders*, ed. Dr. Mohammad-Reza Mohammadi, 2011, www.intechopen.com/books/a-comprehensive-book-on-autismspectrum-disorders/parenting-stress-in-mothers-and-fathers-of-children-with-autism-spectrum-disorders.

3. Michelle Diament, "Autism Moms Have Stress Similar to Combat Soldiers," *Disability Scoop*, November 10, 2009, www.disabilityscoop.com/2009/11/10/autism-moms-stress/6121/.

4. Lisa Smith, "My Response When People Say 'I Don't Know How You Do It,'" *Autism Speaks*, July 15, 2015, www.autismspeaks.org/blog/2015/05/07/response-when-people-say-i-dont-know-how-you-do-it.

5. Smith, "My Response."

6. Mitchell Scott Garry Loepp, "Stress-Related Growth of Parents Raising Children with Autism," Electronic Theses and Dissertations, Paper 5315, July 11, 2015, scholar.uwindsor.ca/cgi/viewcontent.cgi?article=6314&context=etd.

7. Sean González-Lambert, Encarnacion Sarriá, and Beatriz López, "Positive Contributions of Children with Autism to Their Families," *Autism Reseach Network* 15 (April 2015), epub,

www.port.ac.uk/media/contacts-and-departments/psychology/downloads/Issue-15-Positive -Contributions.pdf.

8. Brian Boyd, "Examining the Relationship between Stress and Lack of Social Support in Mothers with Children with Autism," *Sage Journals, Focus on Autism and Other Developmental Disabilities* 17, no. 4 (Winter 2002): 208–215.

9. Marci Wheeler, "Living with Autism, Sibling Perspectives: Guidelines for Parents," Indiana Resource Center for Autism (IRCA), www.iidc.indiana.edu/irca.

10. Maureen Angell, Hedda Meadan, and Julia Stoner, "Experiences of Siblings of Individuals with Autistic Spectrum Disorders," *Autism Research and Treatment* (2012), Article ID 949586, www.hindawi.com/journals/aurt/2012/949586/.

a. Maria Davis, interview with author, September 9, 2015.

b   Shalini Babbar, interview with author, August 3, 2015.

c. Jo Bromley, Dougal Julian Hare, Kerry Davison, and Eric Emerson, "Mothers Supporting Children with Autistic Spectrum Disorders: Social Support, Mental Health Status and Satisfaction with Services," *Autism* 8, no. 4 (December 2004): 409–423.

d. Andrea Pollack, interview with author, October 10, 2015.

e. American Psychological Association, "Understanding Chronic Stress," www.apa.org/help center/understanding-chronic-stress.aspx.

f. Wendy Banner, interview with author, November 1, 2015.

g. Rethink, "Dealing with a Diagnosis–From a Parent's Perspective." www.rethinkfirst.com/ AboutAutism/LivingWithAutism/.

h. Written and submitted by Eli Coopersmith.

i. Dana Fialco, "Five Benefits of Growing Up with an Autistic Sibling," Autism Speaks, www .autismspeaks.org/node/119681.

Chapter 9

1. United States Department of Education, Office of Special Education and Rehabilitative Services, "History: Twenty-Five Years of Progress in Educating Children with Disabilities Through IDEA," www.ed.gov/policy/speced/leg/idea/history.pdf.

2. Lydia Brown, "Identity First Language," *Autistic Hoya* (blog), August 2011, www.autistic hoya .com.

3. Ellen Notbohm, *Ten Things Every Child with Autism Wishes You Knew*, Arlington, TX: Future Horizons, 2012, pp. 101–111.

4. Notbohm, *Ten Things*.

5. M. Catherine Cappadocia, Jonathan Weiss, and Debra Pepler, "Bullying Experiences among Children and Youth with Autism Spectrum Disorders," *Journal of Autism and Developmental Disorders* 42, no. 2 (2012): 266–277.

6. Susan Carter, "Bullying of Students with Asperger Syndrome," *Issues in Comprehensive Pediatric Nursing* 32, no. 3 (2009): 145–154, 151.

7. Catherine Anderson, "Bullying and Children with ASD," Interactive Autism Network, October 7, 2014, iancommunity.org/cs/ian_research_reports/ian_research_report_bullying.

a. Naoki Higashida, *The Reason I Jump: The Inner Voice of a Thirteen-Year-Old Boy with Autism*, New York: Random House, 2013, pp. 45–46.

b.   Lydia Brown, "15 Things You Should Never Say to an Autistic Adult," *Autistic Hoya* (blog), September 2015, www.autistic hoya.com.

The Story of Jake

1.   The term *aspies* has been used in popular culture by those with what was formally known as Asperger's syndrome.
2.   Don Schwartz, "Becoming Bulletproof: The Melding of Two Worlds," *Marin Post*, October 9, 2015, marinpost.org/blog/2015/10/9/becoming-bulletproof-the-melding-of-two-worlds.

Resources

Websites

Autism Research Institute at www.autism.com
Autism Science Foundation at www.autismsciencefoundation.org
Autism Society at www.autism-society.org
Autism Speaks at www.autismspeaks.org
Centers for Disease Control and Prevention at www.cdc.gov/ncbddd/autism/data
    .html
National Autism Association at www.nationalautismassociation.org

Books

An Anthropologist on Mars by Oliver Sacks, 1995
Asperger's Teens: Understanding High School for Students on the Autism Spectrum by
    Blythe Grossberg, 2015
The Autistic Brain: Helping Different Kinds of Minds Succeed by Temple Grandin,
    2014
Autism in Young Adult Novels: An Annotated Bibliography by Marilyn Irwin and
    Annette Goldsmith, 2015
Bright Not Broken by Diane Kennedy and Rebecca Banks, 2011
Carly's Voice: Breaking through Autism by Arthur Fleischmann and Carly Fleisch-
    mann, 2012
*I Am Intelligent: From Heartbreak to Healing—a Mother and Daughter's Journey
    through Autism* by Peyton Goddard and Dianne Goddard, 2012
*Making Autism a Gift: Inspiring Children to Believe in Themselves and Lead Happy,
    Fulfilling Lives* by Robert Cimera, 2007
Mindblindness: An Essay on Autism and Theory of Mind by Simon Baron-Cohen,
    1995
The Reason I Jump: The Inner Voice of a Thirteen-Year-Old Boy with Autism by
    Naoki Higashida, 2013
Ten Things Every Child with Autism Wishes You Knew by Ellen Notbohm, 2006
Thinking in Pictures by Temple Grandin, 2006

Movies

Autism the Musical, 2007. 1 hour, 34 minutes
Becoming Bulletproof, 2015. 1 hour, 20 minutes
A Mother's Courage: Talking Back Autism, 2010. 1 hour, 43 minutes
Temple Grandin, 2010. 2 hours
Wretches and Jabbers, 2010. 1 hour, 30 minutes

Index

ABA. *See* Applied Behavior Analysis

academic ability and outcomes, 2, 4; diversity acceptance and, x; PRT aiding in, 105; range in, 5

acceptance, x, 155, 156, 159, 178–79

acting, 191, 193–94

activities: family, 141, 151, 191; for pretend play, 69; repetitive behavior and diversity of, 7; for sensory diet, 86–88, *87*

ADD. *See* attention deficit disorder

ADHD. *See* attention-deficit/hyperactivity disorder

age: brain size and, *53*, 53–54; of diagnosis, 13–14, 31, 38, 40, 139–40; false beliefs and, 67; medications and, 110; of parents, 50; play stages with, 21; symptoms changing with, 15

aggression, 5, 160

agitation, 9

aloneness, 35

ambivalence, 34

American Psychological Association, 148–49

Anderson, Connie, 177

Angelman syndrome, 61

animals: Grandin's work with, 114, 116, 119–20, 124; phobias of, 29; relationship with, 187

antecedent, 96–97

anticonvulsants, 110

antipsychotic drugs, 110

anxiety: Boyle's, 133–34; fear-based, 185–86; with 9/11, 189; noise creating, 185–86; social support for, 181–82; vestibular system impairment and, 19, 80. *See also* phobias

anxiety disorder, 15, 16

Applied Behavior Analysis (ABA), 162; application of, 92–93; case study of, 97–99; critics of, 99–100; discrete trial teaching in, 95–97, 109; Lovaas's work with, 97–99; pairing in, 94; parents use of, 140, 141; prompts in, 94–97; TEACCH compared with, 108–9; track record for, 92, 100

apraxia, 9

artists, 113

ASD. *See* autistic spectrum disorder

Asperger, Hans, 36–37

Asperger's syndrome, ix, 4, 13, 133; diagnosis of, 6, 37; discovery of, 36–37; friendship and, 127; teasing kids with, 177; terminology for, 193, 204n1

"aspies," 193, 204n1

assumptions, 170, 171

athletics, 176

attention deficit disorder (ADD), 14–15

attention-deficit/hyperactivity disorder (ADHD), 110

auditory function: checklist for, 85; temporal lobe and, 57

autism: Asperger's syndrome and, 36–37; behaviorism and early theories of, 37–38; biological causes for, 43, 50; at birth, 40; coining term for, 33–34; first diagnosis of, 34–36; parents role in theories of, 35, 36, 40–42; psychologists/psychiatrists in history of, 33–45; vaccines in theories of, 43–45

Autism Speaks, 156

Autism Treatment Center of America, 145

The Autistic Brain (Grandin), 42, 76, 115

58–59; peripheral, 18, 25; synesthesia with, 71–72. *See also* eye contact
visual organizers, 107–8
visual processing: brain structure and, 59, 62, 65; continuous, *75*; discomfort with, issues, 19, 25, 31, 75–77, 79; Grandin on, 76, 114–15; teaching and, 107

Wakefield, Andrew, 43–44
Watson, John, 38–39, 40

Williams, Donna, 76
Wimmer, Heinz, 66
Wing, Lorna, 37
World Autism Conference. *See* United Nations World Autism Conference

xir, 173

Zeno Mountain Farm, 193–94

About the Author

Francis Tabone, PhD, is head of school for the Cooke Center for Learning and Development, a school that serves children and young adults from kindergarten to the age of twenty-one with special needs. He has worked to develop programs and models of special education in the multiple schools that Cooke Center runs. Dr. Tabone has been both a teacher and administrator for the Department of Education in New York City, helping to develop innovative programming for special needs students. His work as a teacher, psychologist, and administrator has spanned nearly thirty years.

Dr. Tabone serves as an adjunct professor of special education in several New York colleges and universities. He lives in New York City with his wife and daughter.